HOURGLASS

TIME, MEMORY, MARRIAGE

A MEMOIR

———

DANI SHAPIRO

"Searing . . . a love story through and through." —

"One of the most striking things about *Hourglass* is just how true it rings."   —*Nylon*

"A meditation that's intimate, wide-ranging, funny and smart."   —*Portland Press Herald* (Maine)

"Beautifully drawn. . . . *Hourglass* is a lovely reminder that one of the most profound decisions we make is whom we love and whom we choose to continue to love in a lifetime."   —*Bloomberg*

"With a combination of engaged storytelling and what remains carefully unsaid, Shapiro creates an abstract intimacy that allows the reader into her experience. . . . It is the very book that should be given to a young couple at the beginning of their relationship."
                                              —*Interview*

"Honest and tender. . . . *Hourglass* might already be a classic."   —*Literary Hub*

"In Shapiro's virtuosic hands, time compresses and expands—an accordion playing the sorrowful yet redemptive melody that is life."   —*Brain Pickings*

"An insightful, exquisite deep dive into a marriage."
                          —*The Christian Science Monitor*

Dani Shapiro

HOURGLASS

Dani Shapiro is the bestselling author of the memoirs *Still Writing*, *Devotion*, and *Slow Motion* and five novels, including *Black & White* and *Family History*. Her work has appeared in *The New Yorker*, *Granta*, *Tin House*, *One Story*, *Elle*, *Vogue*, *The New York Times Book Review*, and the op-ed pages of *The New York Times* and the *Los Angeles Times* and has been broadcast on *This American Life*. She has taught in the writing programs at Columbia, NYU, the New School, and Wesleyan University; she is a cofounder of the Sirenland Writers Conference in Positano, Italy. She lives with her family in Litchfield County, Connecticut.

www.danishapiro.com

HOURGLASS

HOURGLASS

Time, Memory, Marriage

Dani Shapiro

ANCHOR BOOKS
A Division of Penguin Random House LLC
New York

Grateful acknowledgment is made to the following for permission
to reprint previously published material:

Alfred Music, Hal Leonard LLC, and Sony/ATV Music Publishing: Excerpt from "Piece
of My Heart," words and music by Jerry Ragovoy and Bert Russell. Copyright © 1967 by
Unichappell Music Inc., Sony/ATV Songs LLC, and Sloopy II Music, copyright renewed.
All rights reserved. All rights on behalf of Sony/ATV Music Publishing LLC administered
by Sony/ATV Music Publishing LLC. All rights on behalf of Sloopy II Music administered
by Wren Music Co., a division of MPL Music Publishing, Inc. Reprinted by permission
of Alfred Music, Hal Leonard LLC, and Sony/ATV Music Publishing.

Counterpoint: Excerpt from "The Country of Marriage" from *The Country of
Marriage* by Wendell Berry. Copyright © 2013 by Wendell Berry.
Reprinted by permission of Counterpoint.

Houghton Mifflin Harcourt Publishing Company: Excerpts from "Could Have" from *View
with a Grain of Sand: Selected Poems* by Wisława Szymborska, translated from the Polish by
Stanisław Barańczak and Clare Cavanagh. Copyright © 1976 by Czytelnik, Warszawa.
Copyright © 1995 by Houghton Mifflin Harcourt Publishing Company. Reprinted by
permission of Houghton Mifflin Harcourt Publishing Company. All rights reserved.

House of Bryant Publications LLC: Excerpt from "Devoted to You" by Boudleaux Bryant.
Copyright © 1958, copyright renewed 1986 by House of Bryant Publications LLC (BMI).
Reprinted by permission of House of Bryant Publications LLC.

The Library of Congress has cataloged the Knopf edition as follows:
Names: Shapiro, Dani, author.
Title: Hourglass / Dani Shapiro.
Description: First edition. | New York : Alfred A. Knopf, 2017.
Identifiers: LCCN 2016029345 (print) | LCCN 2016048566 (ebook)
Subjects: LCSH: Shapiro, Dani—Marriage. | Marriage—Social aspects. | Women novelists,
American—Biography. | Novelists, American—20th century—Biography. | Jewish
women—United States—Biography. | BISAC: BIOGRAPHY & AUTOBIOGRAPHY / Personal
Memoirs. | BIOGRAPHY & AUTOBIOGRAPHY / Women. |
BIOGRAPHY & AUTOBIOGRAPHY / Literary.
Classification: LCC PS3569.H3387 Z46 2017 (print) | LCC PS3569.H3387 (ebook) |
DDC 813/.54—dc23
LC record available at https://lccn.loc.gov/2016029345

Anchor Books Trade Paperback ISBN: 978-1-101-97426-1
eBook ISBN: 978-0-451-49449-8

Book design by Maggie Hinders

www.anchorbooks.com

Printed in the United States of America
10 9 8 7 6 5 4 3 2 1

This book is for M.

Let me fall if I must fall.

The one I will become will catch me.

——THE BAAL SHEM TOV

HOURGLASS

FROM MY OFFICE WINDOW I see my husband on the driveway below. It's the dead of winter, and he's wearing nothing but a white terry-cloth bathrobe, his feet stuffed into galoshes. A gust of wind lifts the hem of the bathrobe, exposing his pale legs as he stands on a sheet of snow-covered ice. His hair is more salt than pepper. His breath makes vaporous clouds in the cold. Walls of snow are packed against the sides of the driveway, white fields spread out to the woods in the distance. The sky is chalk. A rifle rests easily on his shoulder, pointed at the northernmost corner of our roof.

So. He bought the gun. I take a long sip of coffee. Our two dogs are sleeping on the rug next to my desk chair. The old, demented one is snoring. There's nothing I can do but watch as M. squeezes the trigger. *Bam!* I start, and the dogs leap up. The windows rattle. The whole house shakes.

The woodpecker had arrived the previous fall. Once he chose our house he seemed quite content, settled in, as if he had every intention of staying awhile. At first, I had no idea where the noise was coming from. *Rat-tat-tat.* From my study, it sounded like a loose shutter banging, though we had no shutters. It was almost a city sound—like a faraway jackhammer—out of place in the quiet of the country. *Rat-tat-tat-tat-tat.* Of course, it seemed possible, too, that the infernal banging was entirely in my mind. "My head," wrote Virginia Woolf, "is a hive of words that won't settle." I couldn't hold a thought. It was as if an internal axis had been jarred and tilted downward; words and images slipped through a chute into a dim, murky pool from which I could not retrieve them.

Finally, I spotted the woodpecker from my son's bathroom window. Perched on a drainpipe just below the wood-shingled roof, he was a small brown bird with a tiny head and a pointy beak that moved back and forth with astonishing speed as he hammered away at what was already a sizable hole in the side of the house. *Rat-tat-tat.*

· ·

It had been a time of erosion. I'd begun to see in metaphor. We'd lived in the house for twelve years, and things were falling apart. The refrigerator stopped working one day. The banister warped and the spindles on the staircase loosened and clattered to the floor. An old, neglected apple tree on our property split in two, its trunk as hollow as a drum. The house needed painting. The well needed fracking, whatever that meant. The front door was cracked, and on winter days, a sliver of wind could be felt inside.

Late that same fall of the woodpecker, as I sat reading at the kitchen table one afternoon, two large, mangy creatures loped across the meadow. One gray, the other a pale, milky brown, they were otherworldly, terrifying. My spine tingled. I grabbed my phone to take their picture, then texted it to M., who was in the city that day.

Wolves?

No.

Sure?

Yes. Coyotes.

Not coyotes. I know coyotes.

The basement regularly flooded. If the wind blew in a certain way during a heavy rainfall, we could count on a half inch of water in the workroom where M. kept projects in varying states of half-completion. On a long table, he had hundreds of photos cut into

stamp-sized pieces. These, he planned to assemble
into a photo collage. A finished one from years earlier
hangs in our guest bathroom. I never tire of looking at
it: our now-teenaged son as a toddler, hoisted on the
shoulders of a friend, a smiling, radiant man whose
daughter will later fall to her death from a Brooklyn
rooftop; my mother in a hat to cover her bald head,
months before she died; my mother-in-law before
Alzheimer's set in; the three of us—my little family
and I—on the steps of our Brooklyn town house; then
older, on the porch of our house in Connecticut. *Alive.*
Dead. Lost. Like the names I refuse to cross out in my
address book, I catalog those I have loved.

"Honey!" I called downstairs, keeping an eye on the
woodpecker, who, if he noticed me, didn't seem to
care. "I need you!"

M. peered at the woodpecker through the bathroom
window.

"Little fucker."

"I know."

"We're going to have to replace all that siding."

"Let's put it on the list."

The list included pressing items such as painting
the house, fixing the front door. We really did need to
install a generator, replace the heating system. The list
had once included items like redoing the bathrooms,
building an addition. I'd stopped keeping a list.

"I'm getting a gun."

"I don't want a gun in the house."

"Not a real gun. A pellet gun. Nail the fucker."

I did some research. All the while, the pecking continued. More holes were hammered into the side of our house. A friend recommended a brick of suet, hung from a tree. Another suggested a porcelain owl placed atop our roof. M. is not fond of home remedies. The weather grew colder. Leaves on the trees turned russet, deep yellow, bright burgundy. Families of wild turkeys strutted across the front meadow. My mind was on fire. Each day, I sat in my second-floor office and heard *rat-tat-tat-tat-tat*.

I'll take care of it, M. said. A familiar refrain, one I have always loved and long to believe. This longing—my longing—is part of our marriage. We have been together for nearly two decades. The woodpecker, the mangy creatures, the hive of words. The creaky house, the velocity of time, the accretion of sorrow. The things that can and cannot be fixed. *I'll take care of it.*

M., before I knew him, owned *real* guns. He had been a foreign correspondent working out of Africa, in territory that required bodyguards and weapons. He kept a Kalashnikov stored in a locker in Mogadishu.

On occasion, he wore a bulletproof vest. It hangs on a hook in our coat closet.

Now he is having a tête-à-tête with a woodpecker as I stand holding one quivering dog while petting the other. He hadn't listened to me. When had he snuck a gun into the house? Where had he bought it? Walmart? *Bam!* The sound echoes off the roof. His hair is standing on end and he looks not unlike Einstein. A small dark speck against the white sky as the bird flies away, and I can almost hear its laughter, a cartoon bubble: *You can't catch me!*

We have recently embarked on a massive housecleaning after reading a popular book about the Japanese art of tidying up. It falls into the department of things we can control. The author instructs readers to empty the contents of every single household drawer and closet and lay them all out: the old sneakers, balled-up workout clothes, tangled necklaces, single earrings, gift soap still in cellophane wrappers. The report cards, papier-mâché art projects, the Baby Björn. The boxes of heating pads from a long-ago bout with sciatica. The pregnancy test displaying the pink line. The electric s'mores maker, a housewarming gift, deposited unopened in the back of the coat closet.

I found these old journals of yours. Just yesterday, M. handed me two thin spiral-bound notebooks. One is

red, the other blue. They don't look familiar. I open
the red one. Dated June 8, 1997, the entry reads:
*Day one. Arrived early in London and bought books at
Heathrow (paperback ed. of* Angela's Ashes.) *Arrived in
Paris in the early afternoon (Orly) and took a taxi to the
Relais Saint-Germain. D. unpacked. Loved the room,
great big bed, fluffy towels.* My handwriting looks to
me like a letter to my future self, a missive launched
forward through time. If you had asked me if I'd kept
a journal on our honeymoon, I would have told you
with certainty that I had not. And who the hell writes
about herself in the third person in her diary?

*Today we ventured across the Seine only to discover
that the Beaubourg was closed. Went to Agnès B.
where M. bought two nice shirts. Walked through the
Marais, went to Ma Bourgogne, where a pigeon shat
all over the back of M.'s new Agnès B. shirt. D. went
upstairs and washed it off in a public restroom.*

We weren't all that young when we married. I was
thirty-five, M. forty-one. As I read my entries, I feel
time collapsing on itself. It is as if I can reach out and
tap that blissed-out honeymooning not-so-terribly
young woman on the shoulder, point her away from
the fluffy towels and cafés and shitting pigeons, and
direct her toward another screen, a future screen.
As she walks into a shop on the Place Vendôme

(*D. finally ended her search for the perfect watch to go with her beautiful new wedding band*), I want to suggest to her that life is long. That this is the beginning. And that it may be true, at least in poetic terms, that beginnings are like seeds that contain within them everything that will ever happen.

On the highest shelf in my office closet, five boxes filled with reams of pages are stacked along with several cloth-covered volumes from the years I kept journals. Keeping journals was a practice for me, a way of ordering my life. It was an attempt to separate the interior from the exterior. To keep all my trash—this is the way I thought of it—in one place. Into the journals I poured every thought, each uncomfortable desire. Every petty resentment, seething insecurity, unexpressed envy that would be boring to all the world except—perhaps—to me. I continued the journal practice for years after becoming a writer, because I thought of the journals as the place where the detritus would be discarded, leaving only the essential—somehow the process itself would determine which was which—for my *real* work. I never imagined that a soul would read the journals. I would have been horrified, mortified if anyone had seen them. So why are they still on a shelf in my closet? Why have I kept them?

The red and blue notebooks are, I believe, the last

journals in which I wrote. After we returned from our
honeymoon, that practice, which had accompanied me
all through my teens and twenties and into my thirties,
disappeared. It was disappearing even as I wrote
in them, *I* becoming *she*. Interspersed in those thin
notebooks were other things: lists, thoughts, ideas. But
that still doesn't explain why I haven't burned them.
They aren't there for posterity. Nor for reference.
I don't believe the young woman who wrote them
has anything to teach me. What does she know? She
hasn't lived my life.

> *After breakfast we drove to Maussane, home of the*
> *best olive oil in France. Picked up three bottles. Then*
> *left Saint Rémy and took off for the Côte d'Azur.*
> *While in the car, D. ended up getting bitten by a nasty*
> *unidentified flying insect and jumped into the backseat*
> *where she remained crouching until the car stopped.*
> *After determining that the insect was not a bee and D.*
> *would live, we detoured to Aix-en-Provence for lunch*
> *(M.'s idea).*

Some facts: at the moment I write this, I am fifty-two.
M. is fifty-nine. Both ages seem unlikely to me, as
if perhaps I'm making this up. But here we are. We
have been married for almost eighteen years. Our son
is nearly sixteen. We have two dogs, one large, one
small. We have attended twelve weddings, nine bar

or bat mitzvahs, six graduations, five funerals. We
have set foot in twenty-two states, seven countries,
two continents. We have flown one hundred forty-
six thousand miles and easily driven twice that. My
car alone is about to hit two hundred thousand miles
on the odometer. We have held each other's hands
while waiting for biopsy results. We have had a baby
and came very close to losing that baby. We have had
three fights bordering on violent. A handful of terrible
arguments after which we have limped, stunned and
wordless, into our own corners. *Eighteen years*. My
father has been dead nearly thirty years (car accident).
My mother, thirteen (lung cancer). M.'s parents are
still living. His mother has Alzheimer's. His father
can hardly see and strains to hear. He stopped driving
only when his license was revoked. Up until then,
it worked like this: my mother-in-law, blessed with
perfect eyesight but lacking in memory, would let my
father-in-law know when a stop sign was coming
up and read him street names. Together, they drove
that car.

I flip through the second notebook M. found. The blue
one. It is largely empty except for just a few entries
and random scribbled notes from a time during which
M. and I were in the process of buying a Federal town
house in a Brooklyn neighborhood where a young
woman on her way home from work had just been

murdered. The notes are evidence that I had done some research: *On St. Marks this summer there was a body dumped from a car between Carlton and Vanderbilt. She has a whistle and carries it in her fist. Two blocks down, rock thru plate-glass door. The location is in your favor. Feel completely safe.*

Also contained within these pages are lists for the movers (*pack casters with crib, leave changing table contents for Monday*) and notes from interviews with babysitters. Apparently I met with someone named Joan and listed her positive and negative attributes later. *Positive: Washed hands. Knows babies. Lives nearby. Negatives: Evasive. No CPR.*

We lived in that town house for a scant three years before we sold it for what seemed a tidy profit—it is now in one of the most in-demand neighborhoods in New York's most in-demand borough—and decamped for the wilds of Connecticut. By the time we were settled in our new home, my mother was dying. Our son was in preschool. I was turning forty. For my fortieth birthday party—held at the Manhattan loft of my much-older half sister—I had bought what I then considered to be an outfit befitting a forty-year-old: a black silk knee-length skirt and a black cashmere camisole. It seemed life was divided into chapters. In the narrative as I understood it, we were in the early middle.

· ·

An indelible sentence from a short story composed
by a longtime student: "We were young, and in the
reproductive years."

We went back to visit our old house once. We wanted
to show our son, by then a middle-schooler, the home
where he'd spent his toddlerhood. We walked past
the bodega on the corner, once owned by a young
Dominican couple, now transformed into a trendy
restaurant. The journalist who now lives there gave
us a tour. Here was the front door we'd painted dark
green. The buttery yellow walls. The Victorian frosted
glass chandelier. The bright kitchen overlooking the
garden we had planted. Here is where we stood when
we heard the first plane hitting the towers. Here is our
baby in his bouncy seat, wearing a tiny Red Sox cap.
Here I am in my third-floor office, working on a novel.
Oh, and here we are on the floor below, napping in
the master bedroom, the afternoon sun angling across
our bodies, our baby tucked between us. Three chests,
softly rising and falling. And here is the steep, narrow
staircase between the parlor and those bedrooms.
Here is the babysitter—one who had CPR training
and perfect references—slipping near the top step,
dropping our baby as she topples down. Here is the
stoop, the glass doors through which the EMTs race.

Outside, the one-way street down which M. speeds
the wrong way to the hospital, leaning on the horn.
Here, the blue, blue bedroom with a hanging mobile
of circus animals over a blond wood crib. And here,
our baby—miraculously unharmed after a close call.
Here, two parents still young enough to believe that
life holds only one close call per customer.

How do you suppose time works? A slippery
succession of long hours adding up to ever-shorter
days and years that disappear like falling dominoes?
Near the end of her life, Grace Paley once remarked
that the decades between fifty and eighty feel not like
minutes, but seconds. I don't know yet if this is the
case, but I do know this: the decades that separate that
young mother making her lists from the middle-aged
woman discovering them feel like the membrane of a
giant floating bubble. A pinprick and I'm back there.
But is she here? How can I tell her that her lists will
not protect her?

Between us, M. and I have taken on a lot of jobs:
screenwriting, journalism, television writing, book
reviewing, freelance editing, ghost writing, corporate
writing, teaching, leading retreats, public speaking.
Together, we wrote an adaptation of Oscar Wilde's
"The Happy Prince" for an animated HBO series. We

were hired to write an adaptation of my first memoir for a young movie star that landed us on the front page of *The Hollywood Reporter*. As a team, we have taken lots of meetings about lots of projects with lots of people who always appear to be very excited. There were some early years when we would fly home, dreaming of building a swimming pool. There were some years we took our little boy to resorts in warm places. There were some years things worked out. Other years, things didn't. We didn't know that "yes," in Hollywood parlance, meant "maybe" at best. *Use that war reporter shit,* M.'s manager recently told him. *Write what you know, man. I can sell the hell out of that.*

A seventy-year-old student, a retired professor of literature, asks me if I know Wendell Berry's essay "Poetry and Marriage." I do not. The next day, a copy, neatly stapled, is waiting for me on the workshop table. Berry is interested in "the troubles of duration" in the forms of both poetry and marriage. "Form serves us best when it works as an obstruction to baffle us and deflect our intended course. It may be that when we no longer know what to do we have come to our real work and that when we no longer know which way to go we have begun our real journey. The mind that is not baffled is not employed. The impeded stream is the one that sings."

· ·

M. has been documenting our family life since just after our son's birth. In those early months, he made a few short films, and they're loaded on our television along with Netflix and everything else. He's also set our TV so that it plays all of our photos from the last decade—thousands of them—in random order. It's the randomness that's mesmerizing. *Just five more,* we'll sit, transfixed. *Okay, really, now just seven. Ten, and we'll stop.* The jumble of images! At times I'll turn to M. and ask what I'm looking at. Where were we? What was the moment? *That's the roadside place on the way to Taos,* he'll say. Or *that's Judy and Doug's backyard.*

When chronology is eliminated, when life is shuffled like a tarot deck, it's hard to keep track. Was that the summer before last? Whose dining room, what candlelight? I can locate us in time only in one way: by watching our boy growing up.

Tomorrow, Jacob turns sixteen. This is the year that he has changed and grown in ways that have me standing back, gasping with pride, my empty hands aching. He is taller than I am. He's funny and kind. He's strangely good at math. He has a mean backhand. An easy confidence. A shy smile. He still hugs me.

We're deciding on a movie when instead, I ask M. to play one of the early family films. We sit side by side on the sofa in our library, an iced coffee for him, a glass of wine for me, a bowl of pistachios between us. Upstairs, I hear a teenaged boy's laughter as he video chats with his network of friends.

The one M. chooses takes us from our Manhattan apartment to the Brooklyn town house. The soundtrack is bad orchestral baby music that we used to play over and over in an endless loop. Friends stop by. A couple who is now divorced. My mother visits. She will be dead in three years. There is a close-up of two lasagnas bubbling in the oven. Another close-up of the front page of *The New York Times:* TWO YOUTHS IN COLORADO SCHOOL SAID TO GUN DOWN AS MANY AS 23 AND KILL THEMSELVES IN A SIEGE. Now what? Our dog—we put him to sleep the following year—barks and runs around the lobby in slow motion. Then there we are. We both look younger, of course, but it's my baby I'm focused on. My perfect, beautiful baby boy. My eyes sting as I wrap my fingers around M.'s.

The following night we will take Jacob out to a favorite restaurant for his birthday. *Sixteen*. We will give him a video camera—he takes after his father— and at the end of the meal, the owner of the restaurant will bring over a chocolate molten cake pierced by a single candle. *Make a wish*. I watch my son think long and hard. His whole life ahead of him.

"When you see pictures from back then, do you think about what was about to happen—how close we came to losing him?" I ask. "When you see him—"

"Always," M. says quietly.

I often give my students a writing exercise based on a poem titled "Could Have" by the Polish Nobel

Laureate Wisława Szymborska: "It could have
happened. / It had to happen. / It happened earlier.
Later. / Nearer. Farther off. / It happened, but not to
you."

The poet goes on to contemplate the nature of luck.
"You were in luck—there was a forest. / You were
in luck—there were no trees. / You were in luck—a
rake, a hook, a beam, a brake, / a jamb, a turn, a
quarter-inch, an instant."

Write about what could have happened, I tell my
students. What could have happened, but didn't.

Things we brought home from our honeymoon: a
watch, two Agnès B. shirts, three bottles of olive oil,
four pieces of faience pottery from a small village
in Provence. I rarely wear the watch. The shirts
shrunk in the laundry and have long since been given
away. We waited for a special occasion to open the
olive oil. No occasion seemed quite special enough.
After all, we had brought the bottles home with us in
our carry-on. You could do this back then. Finally,
preparing dinner for friends one evening, we opened
one. Of course, it had gone rancid.

The faience pottery is still in perfect condition. A
creamer, a small bowl with scalloped edges, a platter,
a vase—all glazed white, delicately painted with
flowers and vines. I take extra care whenever I handle

them. I remember the sunny day, the Provençal village: *Around Mont Ventoux and along a very intense gorge (no rails, insane French drivers) then through the young lavender fields of Sault and up to Brantes, where this potter works. We really felt as if we had stumbled onto something beautiful.* Someday—perhaps late at night, tired, washing dishes—one will slip through my soapy fingers and shatter. It's only a matter of time.

M. and I are walking down a long empty corridor in the Mark Twain Museum in Hartford, Connecticut, when I hear my name being called from behind us. I turn to see a tall man with a halo of gray hair. He's smiling at me, expectantly. His eyes—it takes me a moment—his eyes are so familiar. *Do I know you?* I can feel M. looking at him, then at me. Back at him, back at me. Suddenly wary. *Who is this guy? Old boyfriend? High school friend? Ex-boss?* Time contracts, and, in an instant, thirty years vanish. I kiss my first husband hello on the cheek. How is it possible that he's in this corridor, in this small museum, a place I have never been before and will likely never be again?

I was just a few years older than my own son is now when I walked down the aisle that first time. I recited vows I couldn't have begun to comprehend. I wore a ring on my finger for just under a year. And then I left. We had no kids, no dogs, no real estate, no shared financial lives. We slid away from one another as easily as two kayaks gliding along the surface of a lake, barely leaving a ripple behind.

"Well, how are you?"

"Good, good. And you?"

The inanity feels like a solid thing, an object we're tossing back and forth like a football. What can we possibly say to each other? *Nice day. Long winter.* I feel M. next to me, waiting to be introduced. So I do. I introduce my two husbands. When he hears the name, M. reacts in a way only I would notice: the quick blink, a slight nod, but otherwise impassive, giving nothing away. He hates surprises. Especially surprises that include ex-boyfriends, ex-lovers. Most of all, surprises that include ex-husbands.

They shake hands, and all my past selves stretch between them like a fragile chain of paper dolls. The nineteen-year-old girl pirouettes over to the fifty-two-year-old woman, her cheeks flushed, arms chubby from the ten pounds she gained freshman year. She has all the self-knowledge of a Labrador retriever. She just wants to grow up, that's all. And she figures marriage will make that happen, as if adulthood is an A.P. course, an item on a to-do list. The fifty-two-year-old has put in the time, but she doesn't have much patience for the girl. She wishes she'd get on with it. Which, of course, is precisely what she did.

· ·

"I think we are well advised to keep on nodding terms
with the people we used to be," wrote Joan Didion
in her essay "On Keeping a Notebook," "whether
we find them attractive company or not. Otherwise
they turn up unannounced and surprise us, come
hammering on the mind's door at 4 a.m. of a bad
night and demand to know who deserted them, who
betrayed them, and who is going to make amends. We
forget all too soon the things we thought we could
never forget."

Husbands. There was not one but two, before M.—
another improbable yet incontrovertible fact. I married
twice. At nineteen, at twenty-eight. Each marriage
lasted less than a year, but there they are. If you type
my name into a search engine, you'll eventually find
the wedding announcements. The first took place at a
country club in Westchester. The second at a rented
mansion on the Upper East Side. I walked down the
aisle in two big white gowns. I said the vows, wore the
ring, sipped the wine. I wanted to be married. Being
married was the point. Deep down, in a place no less
real for being concealed, I carried the knowledge that
I could always get out of it.

When M. and I were first together, I was afraid to
break this news to him. He knew about my second

marriage. But the first marriage—the two marriages—
was hard to explain away. Twice divorced! M. had not
exactly been sitting around waiting for me. There was
the French Sorbonne student, the Polish translator,
the long-suffering semigirlfriend who took care of
his cat when he was off on assignment, the gorgeous
Somali woman who had modeled topless for Peter
Beard. He'd lived with a painter for seven tumultuous
years—way longer than I'd been with both of my
husbands combined.

But there were no wives. He hadn't married.
Something had stopped him. Or else why wouldn't he
have married the painter? It seemed the sacred vows,
the solemn commitment—*for better, for worse, for richer,
for poorer, in sickness, in health, until death do us part*—
had felt more momentous to him than they had to me.

Now—ashamed of my own complicated past—
I waited until we were away for a weekend, and
mustered up my courage to tell him during a long
walk. *I've been married before.* He looked at me,
puzzled. *I mean, twice before.* We stopped walking. We
were miles from our cottage. He took a long while to
respond. *I never thought I'd get married,* he said. *But I
guess I thought that if I did, it would be just as special for
both of us.*

I didn't know how to express to M. that this—us—
was different. Special had nothing to do with the slip

dress by the Belgian designer that I would wear that June, nor the flower-bedecked chuppah draped with my father's tallis. Special was not the Prelude to Bach's Cello Suite no. 1, nor the loin of lamb in the private dining room of the old-school French restaurant. It was not the delicate pavé diamond band of leaves and flowers, nor the Provençal honeymoon. Special was that I had no exit strategy. Special was that I understood I was in it for life, come what may. *For better, for worse.*

After we say goodbye to my first ex-husband, M. and I walk down the empty corridor of the Mark Twain Museum and into the daylight. We drive to the market to pick up groceries for dinner. We're on a familiar route, doing familiar things, but the landscape feels alien. The past—*my* past—has become present. We head home without saying much. I know M. would respond with a shrug if I try to get him to talk about it. *What's there to talk about?* I want to tell him I'm sorry, but that would be ridiculous. M. has always been jealous of my exes. *Would you want me to stop being jealous?* So instead I tell him I love him. To which he responds: *I know.*

I take a selfie in the back of a cab as we idle at a red light on the corner of Fifty-Sixth and Sixth. I raise my

arm, angle my phone from above so that the selfie will
be flattering. I do this perhaps a half dozen times until
I come up with an image I can live with—one in which
I don't look too old, too serious, or like I'm trying
too hard. I've learned that I look best from the left.
Glasses are good, too. And then there are Instagram
filters: *perpetua, willow, ludwig*. I can soften the image,
or sharpen it. Remove shadows, create warmth. When
I've achieved an effect as photoshopped as a women's
magazine cover, I post the selfie on my Instagram feed.
City day. Lunch with an editor, then a friend's book party.
It joins the others: a barn at sunset; a favorite lake;
Jacob hitting a forehand; the big fluffy white dog lying
on a bathroom mat; an empty lecture hall an hour
before I give a reading; the view from a balcony on the
Amalfi Coast where I teach each spring; M. and me in
a dark restaurant in Barcelona.

You've been traveling a lot, friends will say.
Or: *Well, you've had a great summer.*
How was Europe?
Seems like you've been everywhere.

On Twitter, the Literary Hub posts a black-and-white
photo of William Faulkner, tanned, bare-chested,
a pipe in his mouth. He's wearing fashionable sun-
glasses and is sprawled outdoors on a deck, reading

a paperback. His typewriter is in front of him on a low table. The accompanying tweet: *On this day in 1932, Faulkner moved to Hollywood to become a screenwriter; his life looks super chill but it wasn't.*

What doesn't go on Instagram: our bank statements; past due notices; quick glances exchanged when our son isn't looking. Hangovers; sleepless nights; tuition bills. E-mails bearing disappointing news; life insurance forms. Last wills and testaments. Great heaving sighs. The way sometimes we put our arms around each other early in the morning—bleary-eyed, the coffee brewing—and bury our heads in each other's shoulders. *It's going to be okay, right?* The arms tighten. *It's going to be okay.* A shared vocabulary—like a soundtrack to our lives—so familiar that we hardly even notice which of us is speaking. *Eighteen years.*

Not that many years ago, these words I have just used—*Instagram, selfie, tweet, feed*—would have made no sense at all. Just the other day, M. said: "The boy tried to Facetime me while I was I.M.-ing with Trevor." This abbreviated language is the norm. *Tweet. Snapchat. Vine.* Adjectives have become verbs: *I favorited it.* Verbs have become nouns. *How many likes do you have?* Time is moving at such an accelerated rate that completing sentences now seems baroque. My agent's assistant calls to arrange a lunch date. She's *circling back* to *set*. M. leaves word for a producer who is out of the office and will therefore have to *return*.

My father-in-law remembers horse-drawn carriages on the streets of Boston. My mother once spoke of the sky changing color above her New Jersey farm as the *Hindenburg* exploded into flames. I have students who have never mailed a letter, and will never own a watch. When working overseas, M. used to carry a typewriter in a backpack and filed his stories by handing pages to a hotel Telex operator.

At the moment of this writing, I am typing into a laptop keyboard the way I have since I first learned to touch-type the summer of seventh grade on an IBM Selectric. Apparently, using two spaces after a period has become anachronistic. But tell that to my right thumb.

Winter. I am alone in a wooden cottage in the swamplands of eastern Florida, a brief walk from an arts center where I'm spending three weeks as a master artist in residence. When the invitation arrived, I imagined a cottage on a sandy beach, a porch with a hammock, and me in that hammock, swaying slowly in the ocean breeze, a tall glass of iced tea by my side. Perhaps I would read the first two volumes of Knausgaard. Perhaps I would reread *In Search of Lost*

Time. I would get a lot of work done. I would find the thread again.

The walk from my cottage to the arts center where I meet my students each afternoon is along a narrow wooden boardwalk. We are decidedly not on the ocean. The tropical jungle on either side of the boardwalk rustles with wildlife. Later—at the end of my residency—the man who drives me to the airport will tell me about the eighty varieties of snakes he's seen on the property, only two of which are poisonous. But I've managed not to think about snakes. An infestation of carpenter bees at my cottage has my attention. The size of small fists, they swarm each time I open my door. Bees set off in me a seismic reaction, primal, ancient, unreasonable. I'm certain that, if stung, my throat will close up and I will die.

After determining that the insect was not a bee and D. would live, we detoured to Aix-en-Provence for lunch (M.'s idea).

Several years into our marriage, we were at a family picnic with friends in Prospect Park. Juice boxes strewn across a blanket, string cheese softening in the sun, glass containers of baby carrots, bags of healthy chips, toddlers and their plump, sticky hands. The grown-ups sipped wine. I noticed a bee hovering near the rim of my glass. I jumped up, arms flailing, wine

spilling, and M. calmly said—as he had many times—
but you aren't allergic to bees. I became incensed. I
couldn't let it go. He was playing with my life, being
irresponsible, I thought in a white-hot flash. *How do
you know?* I snapped at him. Furious. In front of our
friends. In front of the children.

M. asked me if I remembered that day in Provence.
Of course I did. What was his point? *I lied. It was a bee
that stung you,* M. said. He found it in the back of our
rental car and quickly disposed of it before I could see.
He took matters into his own hands. He knew I would
panic if he told me. *Didn't you wonder why we spent an
hour circling the hospital?*

I'll take care of it, M. says. *I'll take care of it.*

But now—alone, without M., in Florida, miserable—
it doesn't matter what I think, what I know to be true.
I cannot bring myself to leave my cottage and walk
through the swarm. Each morning, I sit at the kitchen
table, pecking away at my laptop. The hot Florida sun
beats against the roof of my cottage and I imagine
them, the fist-sized bees, burrowing into the wood.
I take a break from the essay I'm writing and read up
on their two very different mating systems: large-eyed
males search for females by patrolling, hovering, and
pursuing. Other males release pheromones into the air

while they fly, announcing their presence. *Hey, baby!*
Going my way?

"In English, the term *memoir* comes directly from the
French for memory, mémoire," David Shields offers
in *Reality Hunger*. "And yet more deeply rooted in
the word *memoir* . . . is the ancient Greek, *mermeros*,
an offshoot of the Avestic Persian *memara*, itself a
derivative of the Indo-European for that which we
think about but cannot grasp: *mermer*, 'to vividly
wonder,' 'to be anxious,' 'to exhaustingly ponder.' In
this darker light of human language, the term suggests
a literary form that is much less confident than
today's novelistic memoir, with its effortlessly relayed
experiences."

I tell the carpenter bee story to a friend one evening
when I'm finally back home. I've been telling the
story to whomever will listen, the way one recounts
a trauma. She offers to set up a phone conversation
between me and a man she knows who specializes
in Jungian dream analysis and imagery. In other
words, what do the bees *mean*? Though I no longer
keep journals, I do compile many bits and pieces
of paper on which I take notes. The notes from
the conversation with the Jungian: *Mugged by the
unconscious. Gripped by the hand of god. Phobias are*

fascinations. Shaman-totem-bee. Has the quality of
an initiation. Initiations are in some sense about death.
Initiations are disorienting. Not just to fuck with you,
but to reorient you.

Once in a while, if he's very tired or very drunk, M.'s
Boston roots will reveal themselves. The letter *r* will
vanish. *Smaaaht,* he'll say, for smart. Or *blizzaahd.* He
grew up north of Boston—both his parents speak with
thick, unmistakable New England accents—and that
long-ago boy emerges from the depths of the man, as
if elbowing his way out. *God, I'm hammahed.*

Still there are pockets, absences. Sinkholes inside
my husband where whole other lives are contained—
ones impossible for me to know. His years in Africa
are inaccessible to me. At dinner in Venice, Italy, I
return from the ladies' room to find M. speaking to
the table of tourists behind us in a language I can't
identify. I slide next to him on the banquette and listen
for a moment. The room tilts. Who is this man? What
is he saying? *Kuongea Kiswahili? Mimi aliishi katika
Afrika ya Mashariki kwa miaka kumi na saba.*

That night, we make hard, fast love in our hotel
room. The Swahili has turned me on. My husband
is a stranger. But then morning comes, light seeping
through the windows overlooking the Grand Canal.
M.'s cheek is pressed against the pillow, his eyes
flickering beneath closed lids. I wonder if he's

dreaming of another world. His whole face soft the way it almost never is when he's awake. I watch him breathe. And my own foreign language—the Hebrew of my childhood—returns to me from the distant place inside me where it lives: *Ani l'dodi v'dodi li.* *I am my beloved and my beloved is mine.* And then this: *Hineni,* I silently tell him. *I am here.*

These days, my sleep is disrupted multiple times during the night. It's not insomnia, not exactly. M. has started snoring and so has the old, demented dog—that's some of it. But the feeling is one of being nudged awake at two, three, four in the morning. I lean over to look at the clock. Is it time to get up yet? I lie back down and listen to the snoring. My mind begins to thrum with worry. I compile lists, the kind sure to keep me up until dawn.

For most of my life, I had the persistent sense that I was in a race. Someone—some*thing*—was behind me, gaining on me, and I needed to keep moving in order to outpace it. Outpacing it seemed a viable option. But the longer I have run—and as life has had its way with me—the more I have come to understand the foolishness of running. I married. I had a child. I wove all the threads of myself into a tapestry. I am part of a design. Now I hear a word, *forgive,* echo in my head. The voice isn't mine. More like a wise old crone, insisting: *Forgive.*

But who is it I'm meant to forgive? I hear the first birds call across the meadow. The big fluffy dog stirs, then settles back down, bones hitting the floor in a satisfied thump. The bed creaks as M. turns toward me. Jacob is asleep in his room on the other side of the staircase, door closed, the multicolored plastic sign we purchased for a four-year-old in a souvenir shop announcing JACOB'S ROOM still glued to the paint.

What must we summon and continue to summon in order to form ourselves toward, against, alongside another person for the duration? To join ourselves to the unknown? What steadiness of spirit? What relentless faith?

As dawn streaks pink across the sky, the crone's words land. It's *us*. I understand. M. and me. It's us I need to forgive.

"A mosaic," writes Terry Tempest Williams, "is a conversation between what is broken."

In crafting a work of fiction, at least in first draft, a writer's got to have a kind of willful blindness to her own motivations. Why the knock at the door, the chance meeting, the near miss? The writer may not know, even as she proceeds. But when the self—not a fictional character—is the landscape of the story, we can't afford to be blind to our own themes and the strands weaving through them. And so we must make a map, even as the ground shifts beneath us.

This is, of course, not only a literary problem.

After our housecleaning, we still had a few rooms that remained untouched. We kept waiting for a rainy weekend to tackle the basement, which, M. would argue, ought to be next on our list. But I found it overwhelming. The basement requires a Dumpster, or at the very least a pickup truck to haul stuff away.

It was easy to part with the contents of closets and drawers—the old sweaters, jeans, dresses, boots. The gold satin dress by the Italian designer, worn to a friend's black-tie wedding (they now have twins in first grade), the scraped-to-shit pans, broken thermometers, stained dishtowels. But to get rid of my mother's sister's china, for instance, is to cut loose the hopeful young woman who chose the pattern decorated with cheerful bursts of gold and silver confetti. To tape up that box and cart it off to Goodwill kills her all over again. Or perhaps this is sentimental and foolish. She's dead, dead, dead.

Rainy weekends come and go. The basement remains an obstacle course of boxes. I can't part with the framed diplomas of my parents and their siblings. They were the first generation in my family to go to college. How does *that* get tossed in a Dumpster? My uncle's pipe, my aunt's forty-year-old golf clubs,

ceramic figurines from my grandmother's apartment
in her assisted-living facility mingle as if at a family
reunion with Jacob's discarded booster seats and board
games. I am an only child. I have inherited it all.

M. goes down there, once in a while, and hauls up
a few boxes filled with long plastic containers of slides.
There are thousands and thousands of them, mostly
from my parents' vacations, and they'll be ruined soon
if not already. He sifts through them and digitizes
the ones with people in them. These are few and far
between.

"What we have," he tells me, "are endless Alps."

The pharmaceutical company calls after reading
some of my work in *The New Yorker*. They're in the
late stages of clinical trials for a drug that shows great
promise in slowing the progression of Alzheimer's.
Might M. and I be interested in writing something
for them? Something—they have no idea what—
that will create empathy and dramatize the effects of
Alzheimer's on a family? We know something about
the effects of Alzheimer's on a family.

Big Pharma! It's all very hush-hush. Very cloak-
and-dagger. We sign a nondisclosure agreement—
perhaps I am breaking it now—before we meet with
them. Writing for a pharmaceutical company isn't
something either of us has imagined doing. But ever
since the Writers Guild strike, the invisible rule book

for screenwriters has changed. M. is having trouble
getting projects off the ground. He recently pitched
an idea to one of the Hollywood studios. They loved
it and promised to get behind it, once he brought them
a script, a star, and a director. This puzzled M., who
asked: *But if I have a script, a star, and a director, why
do I need you?*

The rule book for literary novelists has also
been revised. Writing books—even quote-unquote
best sellers—is no longer a way to make a living.
I've caught myself wondering whose job it is to name
nail polishes. *Gucci Mucci Pucci. I Pink I Can. Berry
Naughty.* The driveway needs repaving. We have to
replace the siding, thanks to Mr. Woodpecker. *Of
course,* we tell the pharmaceutical company. *Create
empathy. We know how to do that.*

We propose that we write a play about a man who
develops Alzheimer's and the ripple effect of the
disease on his family, friends, and community. We
offer to cast and produce the play ourselves. The
play—more like an elaborate staged reading—will be
performed during a daylong event for executives in
other companies with whom they hope to eventually
partner. They agree to the fee we quote them, which
is enough to keep us going for half a year, and maybe
even finally get the house painted.

M. and I work very hard by any standard. No, writing
is not the same as repairing power lines in the middle

of a blizzard. Writing does not compare with military deployment. We have—I'm sure we can all agree—First World problems. Or whatever you want to call them. But nonetheless, we have always worked pretty much seven days a week, and every waking hour. We work in bathrobes, barefoot, not even taking the time to shower or dress in the morning. Our vacations are entirely work-related. It turns out that two writers being married to each other is perhaps not the most practical way of going through life. We have no savings, no retirement plan. Some months we are barely able to pay our bills and triage them until the next check comes in. We have nothing to fall back on but each other. Our minds are always churning. *What next?* We wonder. *What next?*

For years now I have been keeping small, special notebooks into which I write passages that strike me hard as I read the work of others. Perhaps these are another form of diary. Certainly, they are deeply personal. I hadn't known, when I started this practice, that these are sometimes called commonplace books. The notebooks I've chosen for this task fit into the palm of my hand, and into the back pocket of my jeans. I've become quite attached to them and order a few at a time from Japan. It takes me years to fill even one. For my tiny script to later be legible, I must write slowly and carefully. The criterion is that the words must pierce me, stop me, so that I can go no further until I write them down—until I make them mine.

You could say these are a record of my life.

Alas, the heart is not a metaphor—or not only a metaphor, Elizabeth Hardwick writes in *Sleepless Nights.* On the next page, a line from Seamus Heaney: *It steadies me to tell these things.*

It turns out that M. and I were both right about the strange animals who loped through our meadow—the otherworldly ones, the sight of which shot a tingle up my spine.

Wolves?

No. Coyotes.

Not coyotes. I know coyotes.

I've seen the creatures a half-dozen times. They seem to show up only when I'm home alone. The gray one is large and boney. The milky brown one is smaller, though more muscular, and looks to be injured. It (she?) moves slowly, dragging her hind leg. One never appears without the other. Are they siblings? A couple?

One evening, at dinner with friends, the subject comes up and I pull out my phone, scroll through photos until I find a series I took of the pair.

"Oh," our friend says, peering at my phone's screen. "Those are coy-wolves."

"Coy-wolves?"

Now he has M.'s attention.

"Hybrids. Somewhere along the line, a coyote and a wolf bred, probably generations ago."

"So now it's a thing?"

"Yeah, it's definitely a thing. There was just a documentary about it."

Back home, M. finds the documentary on Netflix and we settle into our usual spot in the library. The television's blue light reflects us against the panes of the glass doors: a husband and wife curled up together beneath a worn, nubby blanket.

Coy-wolves are everywhere. They've been found in Pennsylvania and Ohio. They've traveled south from New England through the Appalachian Mountains to Virginia. Footage shows coy-wolves in Manhattan and its northern suburbs. Cameras equipped with night vision have caught them scrounging for scraps in Dumpsters, moving in packs across parking lots. I think of the sounds I sometimes hear late at night, far off—or so I like to think—in the woods beyond our meadow. The *yip-yip-yip* of a pack of coyotes circling its prey.

M. and I, together in the library, the documentary over, stare out into the darkness. I wonder if our coy-wolves—I now think of them as ours—are out there now. Even their voices are something new to this world; living creatures making sounds that have never before existed. Perhaps the smaller, injured one had been caught in a trap, or attacked.

Her companion won't leave her. They're a couple,
I decide.

That first winter after we moved from Brooklyn to
Connecticut, a local high school senior lost control of
his car on a winding road as he drove to school with
his brother. I learned of the accident only because
there were roadblocks near the village green on the
day of the funeral, and ashen-faced cops, probably
only a year or two older than the boy, directing traffic.

Baldwin Hill Road—where the accident occurred—
is one of the prettiest I've ever seen. At the top of the
hill, if you look west, is an old cemetery, and beyond
the weathered, simple tombstones, a church steeple
soars in the distance. I've driven it most days for the
past twelve years. When Jacob entered preschool, it
was the route we took early each morning, sometimes
stopping for juice, a bag of chips, or a coffee for me
along the way.

It was autumn when I first saw the mother. She
knelt in the dirt next to the electrical pole the boy had
hit. She wore jeans and a sweatshirt, long hair tied
back, hands working the earth. I knew instantly that it
was her. I slowed my car down, worried—she wasn't
far off the side of the road and could easily be hit by
a texting driver. But I didn't stop. Her bowed head,
those grasping hands seemed to exist on another plane,
a scorched landscape of grief that forced a shudder

through me. I had come so close to knowing that precise grief. Instead, my little boy and I continued on our way.

Month after month, I kept an eye out for the mother as I drove Baldwin Hill. On a number of occasions, I spotted her crouched by the electrical pole. But it wasn't until early spring, when we passed a soft blur of yellow one morning, that I realized what she had been doing in that roadside dirt. Daffodils ringed the pole, encircling the spot where her son died.

All sorts of flowers now mark that spot. Sometime during the first few years, I noticed her sitting one afternoon in a folding chair, her back to the road. Each winter, as the bulbs she plants in autumn sleep in the earth, she strings tinsel around the pole, red and silver glitter hugging its circumference. Once, a nearby tree was festooned with Christmas lights.

Twelve years. Our town has changed quite a bit in these years. More young families have moved up from the city—telecommuting making possible a different kind of life. I see the new moms sometimes. I know them from their SUVs and station wagons, a whole new generation strapped into booster seats in back. They, too, drive up Baldwin Hill. They, too, stop for juice, chips, and coffee. I doubt they notice the one electrical pole set apart from the others by the flowers blooming at its base.

· ·

In crafting a work of fiction, a writer has to choose among calamitous events. There is no value in piling on. This kind of piling on—a rookie mistake—might well come across as melodramatic. Do we really need the plane crash *and* the heart attack? The arson *and* the cancer? Choose one, or risk straining the reader's credulity. The reader of fiction is, after all, in the very delicate process of suspending her disbelief. She is likely engaged in an unarticulated and unconscious hope that the writer will keep things relatively simple, at least as relates to the machinations of plot: disaster is meted out at a tolerable tempo.

Autumn in the year 2000. M. and I are settled in the Federal town house with our six-month-old baby. Together, we are adapting my first memoir for the young movie star in our side-by-side offices. Money is—for the moment—not a problem. We hire the babysitter with perfect references and CPR training. *Time Out* sends a photographer and features our home in an issue. I found the magazine during our basement cleanup and have just now brought it to the framers: our high-ceilinged living room, sunny bedroom, elegant marble fireplaces. The two of us—me with my new-mom haircut, my belly still soft with baby weight, M. looking young, handsome, and in control—sitting in the garden below. Our life—captured in the pages of the magazine—is charmed.

Then the babysitter slips and falls. Our baby hits his head. But before this—before this—something has already gone terribly wrong inside him, though we don't yet know it. Just days earlier, I had seen a flicker in his eyes that made my blood turn to ice. The doctor—too busy to see him—was unconcerned. But the doctor was wrong. The fall is child's play. The two events that happen one on top of the next—*bam, bam!*—are not connected. The fall—the bump on his skull, the fear of concussion, of internal bleeding—is *nothing*. In fact, it is a gift. Now the doctors are paying attention.

Soon we have a diagnosis. A rare disease: *West's Syndrome. Infantile Spasms.* Words so alien they aren't even terrible, not at first. Spasms. Infantile. That doesn't sound so bad. But it is bad—dire, in fact. Most babies don't survive, and if they do, suffer brain damage. We spend the next year, the odds stacked heavily against us, in our magazine-worthy home, struggling with rewrites of our Hollywood script, medicating our baby every four hours around the clock, not knowing if he will live or die.

Marriages often don't survive something like this. The thought came as M. and I drove home to Brooklyn from the neurologist's office, our terribly sick son asleep in his car seat behind us. It was a strange thought, profoundly unhelpful, one of many in a cascade, all white-hot, searing. Faced with the prospect of losing my child, the pain I felt at the notion that my marriage would be tested was dulled, blunted, as if I were being repeatedly stabbed with a butter knife.

I looked over at M. as we crossed the bridge. His hands were tight against the steering wheel, and he was blinking rapidly. I wanted to reach out, to tell him everything was going to be okay, but I knew no such thing, and I was afraid if I moved even a fraction of an inch I might disintegrate. I wasn't sure I was real. I wasn't sure *this*—any of it—was real. How well did I know my husband? We'd fallen for each other the moment we met; spent almost every night together after our first date; married after seven months; had a baby two years into our marriage. We were innocents. We were in the infancy of us.

> *After breakfast—and a walk to buy chocolates at Gérard Mulot—we went to the Gare de Lyon and took the TGV to Avignon. Avignon was very hot. Got into the (air-conditioned) rental car and drove to Crillon le Brave. Gorgeous spot. We were happy to be there. Unpacked (D. again) and went down to the pool. Discovered D. forgot her bathing suit. Had some cheese. Unwound. Stayed at Crillon for dinner, which was delicious, outside on the terrace. M. began his Provençal quest to consume an entire lamb before we left.*

· ·

Sometimes now, I will watch M. through the window as he runs the dogs, or as he walks along a city street in my direction, before he's seen me waiting. His hair has gone mostly white, and he's twenty pounds heavier than when we met. Almost always, he wears jeans and dark sweaters, and either boots or sneakers. On his left wrist, the watch I gave him for a long-ago birthday. His platinum wedding band is on his ring finger. *Eighteen years*. My parents were nearing their thirtieth anniversary when my father died. My in-laws have reached their sixtieth.

In a foreign city, M. and Jacob walk ahead of me, shoulder to shoulder. I trail a few steps behind, blending in with the crowd, enjoying the sight of them. For all the years of his childhood, Jacob looked just like me. At sixteen, he looks like his father. He's very affectionate, especially for a teenager, and sometimes as they walk they'll put their arms around each other.

I am no longer consumed by the question: *What if?* What if I hadn't noticed the infinitesimal seizures? What if Jacob hadn't fallen down the stairs? What if I hadn't noticed the seizures *before* Jacob had fallen down the

stairs? What then? In how many ways would I have
blamed myself for hiring the wrong babysitter, moving
to Brooklyn, living in a four-story home, having a
staircase? What if the drugs hadn't worked? What if
M. and I had disagreed on a course of action? There
were choices to be made. What if M. and I had seen all
this differently?

Never once during that year did we exchange a cross
word, an insult, an intimation of blame. Never once
did we disagree—when faced with monumental
decisions—about what to do. What if the *us* of us
had burnt up in all the terror? Instead, we cleaved
together and became stronger. This, we shared.
For better, for worse.

Ever since M. and I have been together, I have been
drawn to the marriages and the work of literary
couples: Elizabeth Hardwick and Robert Lowell;
Sylvia Plath and Ted Hughes; Joan Didion and John
Gregory Dunne; Jane Kenyon and Donald Hall.
Some of these did not end well. But some—when
they did—strike me as partnerships of immeasurable
beauty.

   Donald Hall describes the rhythm of daily life on
his family farm during his twenty-three-year marriage
to the late poet Jane Kenyon: "We did not spend our

days gazing into each other's eyes. We did that gazing when we made love or when one of us was in trouble, but most of the time our gazes met and entwined as they looked at a third thing. Third things are essential to marriages, objects or practices or habits or arts or institutions or games or human beings that provide a site of joint rapture or contentment. Each member of a couple is separate; the two come together in double attention. Lovemaking is not a third thing but two-in-one. John Keats can be a third thing, or the Boston Symphony Orchestra, or Dutch interiors, or Monopoly. For many couples, children are a third thing."

Later in the essay, he adds: "Sometimes you lose a third thing."

My parents had three marriages between them before they met. My father had been divorced by his first wife and lost his second wife to cancer. My mother had married young and was divorced at twenty-nine. They married each other in a last-chance kind of way, and stuck together like two people who had run out of options. *Thirty years.* Whatever hope might have accompanied their early years quickly devolved into mutual disappointments and bitterness.

They did not have a third thing—not even me.

They were each lost—to themselves, to each other—
before I was born. Thirty years is a long time to go
through the motions. I try to visualize the home
we shared. Images materialize, as if from an under-
exposed photograph. A round, white table, very
midcentury modern; I wish I still had it. Objects:
two telephones, side by side; newspaper clippings; a
jumble of folders; scraps of paper on which lists were
written in my mother's distinctive, vertical script.
I summon the sound of the garage door opening, the
whistle of a kettle, the clink of glass milk bottles, our
small poodle's paws clattering excitedly against the
floor. But I can't summon an image of my parents
together. Not side by side at a recital, a school play, a
graduation. Not taking a walk. Not lying around reading the Sunday paper.

On my shelf of journals, I have kept a few notebooks of my mother's that I found in her apartment
after she died. From a thin, scarlet one with gold-
embossed NOTES AND ASSIGNMENTS on the cover,
she appears to have transcribed some comments made
to her by my father, dated September 18, 1981: *I should
have thrown you out of the house years ago. You don't
hear yourself. You drone on and on.* Later, she writes:
Memories: I was once important. What have I done?

Moments appear like scattered puzzle pieces. What
belongs to what? Where are the corners? I can hold
only bits and pieces in my hands, and even these
are suspect. I can't bring my parents close. It's not

possible to sit them back down again and ask them:
What happened? Did you ever love each other?
When did you stop? Your legacy is a daughter who
tries and tries to remember you.

"Without the binding force of memory," observed
the neurobiologist Eric R. Kandel, "experience would
be splintered into as many fragments as there are
moments in life."

My mind turns once again to the tangible: my own
stacks of journals, the lists scrawled in notebooks.
Wittgenstein makes an appearance in my commonplace book: "All I know is what I have words for."

To do:
1. *Magician*
2. *Party favors!*
3. *Poster*
4. *Call Dena re bill paying, etc.*
5. *Dr. Chachua re hospice care*
6. *Christine at Knopf re travel*
7. *Cake for J*
8. *Call Shelly (Mom's accountant)*
9. *Cancel Hilary's visit*
10. *Balloons (Enchanted Forest)*

I finally clear out the one room in our house that
has no purpose. It would have been a second child's
room, had we had a second child. Instead, a daybed,

a cumbersome French antique, is pushed up against one wall. It's too small for guests to sleep in, though I sometimes stumble from my own bed, driven out by M.'s snoring, and curl up in it. On the floor, a pile of extra prayer books left over from Jacob's bar mitzvah three years ago. Paintings and photographs are hung haphazardly on the walls.

One afternoon, like a crazy person, I don't stop until the walls and floor are completely bare. It becomes pure emptiness, a blank page, waiting for whatever comes next. Something about the room being swept clean pleases me. It stays like this for a while. The wide-plank floors shine in the dappled northern light. The windows are unadorned. The walls, plain. But eventually something seems to be missing. The room has decided: it wants to have a purpose.

In the basement, M. reminds me, we have a heavy iron platform made for a narrow futon. We even have the futon itself, though it has been rolled up for a dozen years, and there is evidence that it has been home to generations of baby mice. We lug the metal frame up two flights, have a piece of thick plywood cut to fit it. In the city one day, I buy a new futon.

After I unroll it, I sit down in the center of the simplest room in my house. The idea is that I will close the door and meditate in this room. I will keep out the encroachments of work and family life. It will be the place where my mind grows still and quiet.

My meditation practice starts with a series of blessings. *May I be safe. May I be happy. May I be strong. May I live with ease.* The practice involves offering these blessings or wishes first to myself, then to a series of others: a benefactor or teacher, a beloved person; then on down the line: a familiar stranger, an enemy or difficult person, then finally, all living beings, near and far.

M.'s mother appears in my meditation. I see her gray, chin-length bob. Her shiny, lacquered nails. I can almost fold her in my arms. The progression of her Alzheimer's has been mercifully slow. But now, my once sharp and crusty mother-in-law can't hold on to a thought. Conversations with her cover only a very small amount of ground before she begins loop back to where she started, the loops ever tightening. Her eyes—so like M.'s—have become faded, foggy. She shuffles when she walks.

But one thing hasn't changed. Her disease may have robbed her of even the faintest hold on the everyday, but she has lost nothing when it comes to whom she loves. She recognizes perfectly well each of her children, every one of her six grandchildren. She knows that she adores her husband. "What can I tell you?" she'll say. "I'm still crazy about the sonofabitch."

Together they have raised three children, built a business from nothing, made some money, lost it, then recovered once more. They've traveled the world. They've had terrible fights and they've made up. "We take it a day at a time," she always says now. One of her loops. "At our age, what else are you going to do? We still have each other." *Sixty years.*

From time to time, I type my own name into Google. I search for answers to many questions on the Internet. As I often tell my students, show me your search history and I will show you your obsessions. *To vividly wonder. To be anxious. To exhaustingly ponder.* A quick perusal of my recent search history includes carpenter bees, Carl Jung, roasted cauliflower, No.6 clogs, coy-wolves, woodpeckers, pellet gun, Citizens of Humanity jeans, White Moustache Yogurt, Alzheimer's, futon, Aristotle's *Poetics*, yoga in Miami, restaurants in Barcelona, *Dame* magazine, Literary Hub, Nike Tennis Camp, Italo Calvino, and fingerless gloves.

It's only when I'm traveling—away from home, away from M.—that I tend to search for myself. As if I need to keep tabs on my whereabouts. As if this is a valid way to be sure I still exist. On a trip to Minneapolis, alone in my hotel room, I scroll through mentions on blog posts, online magazines, news items about that evening's reading at a literary center.

To the right of the screen, a patchwork of images, author photos, mostly. Here's one, taken by M. a few years ago at a crowded café in Rome. I'm glancing away from the camera and my hands are clasped, in view. My wedding ring—*D. finally ended her search for the perfect watch to go with her new wedding band*—is clearly visible. A delicate platinum-and-diamond vine, it broke into two pieces on that trip, as it had several times before. It really was—the jeweler herself told me—too fragile a piece of jewelry to wear every day.

Below the photos, the search engine helpfully lists my vitals: where I was born, went to school, a few of my books. It gets some things wrong, or at least misplaces emphasis. I don't much care, or even pay attention. But then I see a photo of M. It's a black-and-white portrait, taken on the same day that a friend shot us for our wedding announcement. Beneath it, the caption reads: *Ex-spouse.*

I sit on my bed, stunned and panicked. I'm due back at the literary center—my students are waiting and I have a busy afternoon and evening ahead of me—but this news has pinned me to the spot. I type M.'s name into the search engine, hoping for different information. Sure enough, under his photo, there I am, listed as his former spouse. I call M. at home in Connecticut.

"Google has divorced us," I say.

We're at a benefit at Alice Tully Hall in which celebrities have been asked to read the work of poets. The final reader of the evening is Kris Kristofferson. I had a crush on him when I was a teenager, and I've been watching him from my seat in the third row. According to the program, he's supposed to read a William Blake poem.

Instead, Kristofferson is helped slowly across the stage and plugs his guitar into the amplifier. No poem, then. It shouldn't come as a shock, I suppose, that Kristofferson is an old man, close to eighty. He has the same great craggy face, and it's not a stretch to see the heartthrob just beneath the surface. I feel M.'s leg pressed against mine as we listen to him tune up and begin to play.

Busted flat in Baton Rouge, waitin' for a train . . .

The crowd explodes. There's something electric about the iconic song being sung by the man who wrote it, one so frail now he needed help lifting his guitar and strapping it on. His voice cuts through decades like a saw through a tree trunk. Kristofferson's on-again off-again lover, Janis Joplin, died just days after recording "Me & Bobby McGee." How many thousands of times has he sung "Me & Bobby McGee" through the years? He has said that every time he sings it, he thinks of her.

I steal a glance at M. He's looking straight ahead. I know what he's thinking. M. spent most of a year working on the screenplay for a biopic of Joplin. Project after project had crashed and burned, but all the signs looked excellent for this one: The money had been raised by a passionate producer. M. had brought in an Oscar-winning director. A movie star with singing chops had signed on. During that time, I felt a secret, thrilling vindication. *Finally, finally,* went the song in my head. I'd always held fast to the belief that things would work out for M.—for us. That we'd be able to take a step back from the edge. In recent years, I had scrambled to pay the bills as M.'s career took some hits. It had begun to wear on me.

I grab M.'s hand as we listen to Kristofferson thrum the last cords of "Bobby McGee" on his acoustic guitar. The Joplin project fell apart, though occasionally a rumor flies around that Courtney Love is now attached, or Renée Zellweger, or Melissa Etheridge. Whatever happens, he will no longer be a part of it. Where does hope go when it vanishes? Does it live in a place where it attaches itself to other lost hopes? And what does that place look like? Is it a wall? A sea? Is it the soft bafflement I sometimes see in my husband's eyes?

During the time M. lived in the world of putting that film together, Janis sang the sound track to our lives. That tragic, troubled, brilliant young woman who blazed, then went dark, like a meteor—she was with us wherever we went. She pleaded with us through our car's speakers as we drove the hills of Connecticut. She became the ring tone on M.'s cell phone. *Didn't I make you feel like you were the only man? Didn't I give you everything that a woman possibly can?*

· ·

From the shelf of journals: a hardbound cloth diary with a vintage botanical butterfly print inset on its cover. The endpapers are an elegant gray and display an ornate crest surrounding the words: *Labor Omnia Vincit*. Work conquers all. There was indeed a time in my life when I had come to believe that work—not love—conquered all. Beneath the crest, in a deeper gray: *Made in Italy exclusively for Cavallini & Co. San Francisco*. Perhaps it was a gift. Or maybe I bought it for myself with the best of intentions.

The journal seems brand-new, untouched. The spine cracks when I open it. On the first page is a single entry, dated April 30, 1996, shortly after I had signed a contract to write a memoir. *Where on earth do I begin? Do I cut back and forth in time, as I am inclined to do in my fiction? Do I tell the story chronologically and try to make linear sense of it? Or do I allow it to be a patchwork of moments? Do I incorporate the very idea of writing a memoir into the memoir itself—the fear of exposure, of hurting people I love, of finding out things I don't know—or don't know I know? How much of the truth do I tell?*

I'm in an airport in Colorado with M. and Jacob. We've just spent the past week in Aspen—a working vacation—where I taught at a conference. Each morning, at a little before nine o'clock they'd

leave—for breakfast, a hike, a walk into town—
and my students and I would begin our deep dive
into the manuscripts of the day. Particularly in
memoir workshops, the stories themselves are often
wrenching: a kidnapping in South Africa; an uncle
convicted of murder; a husband's betrayal; a son's
suicide.

We speak of the writer not as *you* but, rather, *she*.
We don't get caught up in the events themselves, but
instead focus on the order and shape, the larger sense
the writer is trying to make out of what has happened.
We are engaged in "the monumental task," as Vivian
Gornick tells us in *The Situation and the Story,* "of
transforming low-level self-interest into the kind of
detached empathy required of a piece of writing that
is to be of value to the disinterested reader." While
in Aspen, I was on a panel one evening with Andre
Dubus III, who spoke of what happens when a
memoir devolves into self-pity: "Wah, wah, wah.
Should we call the wambulance?"

But the delicacy of the operation has taken a lot
out of me, and by the time we're at the airport, I'm
pretty well depleted, and nearly in tears myself. My
students' stories linger inside me. And now, M. and
Jacob are flying off in one direction, and I'm flying off
in another. There are storms in Denver, high winds.
The whole thing feels impossible. M. and I take a walk
around the airport. I don't want Jacob to see me cry.

"I don't like this. I wish we were all flying
together."

"Me too." By which I know M. simply means he wishes we didn't have to part—not that he has visions of one of our planes crashing into the Rockies.

"I need to get back to my writing," I say to M.

"I know, baby."

"Tell me everything's going to be okay."

M. hates it when I ask him this. But I am childlike, borderline petulant, needing any kind of reassurance, even the false kind.

"Everything's going to be okay," he echoes.

I'll take care of it.

We pass an airport spa—a twenty-first-century invention. Travelers are being massaged, their faces in cradles, backs vulnerable, suitcases by their sides.

"You're doing really good work."

My mood lifts slightly. I show M. pages in process, even these. He's stingy with praise, my toughest critic.

"I do have one comment," he says.

Now I gird myself. M. has told me he's fine with my writing about him—about us—but I don't know. Maybe all this is getting a little too close for comfort.

"You're making me out to be too good a guy," he says. "I mean, I'm okay. But you need to be harder on me."

How did you meet? A favorite question among couples who are getting to know each other. Ask any longtime couple and they will launch into their routine.

We met through friends. At a party. In school. On Match.com. Over years, these answers tend to become as synchronized as dance moves. *Honey, do you want to tell the story? Or shall I?* Still, the question continues to be asked. Perhaps it's our unconscious way of urging one another to revisit that distant, shimmering moment in which we first began.

"At a Halloween party," M. says.

We're out with new friends. Instead of waiting for the inevitable next question, I jump in.

"We weren't in costume."

"We aren't costume people," M. says.

"It was the day after Halloween, actually. Down near Gramercy Park."

In the dim clatter of the restaurant, I am for a moment transported back to that crowded party. The introduction made by a journalist friend: *Dani, have you met M.?* I suppose M. and I shook hands. He was wearing a black sweater. Our eyes met and—neither years nor memory have altered this fact—I thought: *There you are.*

"It was a literary party," M. says airily.

I feel a flash of annoyance. Is he trying to impress the couple across the table? What does it matter that it was a literary party? An almost imperceptible layer of fear has slowly settled over M. like a thin net. I have been watching him carefully, too carefully. How is he going to contend with these last few years of disappointment? He's nearly sixty. When we first met,

a jumble of awards for his war reportage occupied
a corner of his desk. Then he changed course and
became part of a long tradition of journalists-turned-
screenwriters. Neither of us was expecting that this
was what sixty would look like.

"M. had just gotten back from Somalia that day,"
I rush on. I leave out the fact that he had been
ambushed on his way to the airport in Mogadishu.

"I walked around the block three times," M. says.
"Finally I bought a bottle of scotch and went in."

"And I was supposed to be in L.A.," I say.
"I decided at the last minute to cancel the trip."

We continue this way, revisiting and revising the
myth of us. Marveling at the odds that the whole
thing could have been a near miss. *There you are.*
My mother-in-law told me, years later, that M. had
called the next morning and told her he'd met the
woman he was going to marry.

After dinner, we bid our new friends good night
on a street corner, then walk to the garage where our
car is parked. *Eighteen years.* It hadn't been a great
evening. M. seemed out-of-sorts, flat and disaffected.
There are times when I look at him, and it is as if he
has fled the premises. I can read his mood like the
weather in a wide western sky. When I ask what's
wrong, his responses vary: "I'm working," he'll
say. "I can't just turn it off the way you do." On
occasion—feeling cornered—he'll snap. "I don't
know what you're talking about."

The couple had asked M. a question that often comes up when we tell the story of how we met. *Do you miss Africa?*

"Sure, I miss it. But I met Dani and never went back."

"Never? Were you tempted?"

"One time, after we were married. An editor called from *Outside* magazine. They wanted to send a writer into the Congo."

"On a Red Cross plane," I interjected. "Nobody else was flying in."

"To report on missing Rwandan refugees."

He glanced at me. "It's no job for someone with a family. A lot of my friends were killed. I was getting too old for it."

What he doesn't say is that I didn't want him to go. When he hung up the phone after talking to the editor I could see his eyes lit with excitement. What did he see reflected back at him? Fear. He saw fear. A fault line within me trembled—it felt impossible— as I imagined him alone, in danger, away from me. Out of reach.

He survived the ambush. Circled the block. Bought the bottle of scotch. Told himself he'd stay five minutes. I canceled my trip to L.A., along with a blind date with a Hollywood agent. *Dani, have you met M.?* We are a middle-aged couple driving home to Connecticut. Two hours to the north, a boy sleeps on his bottom bunk in a room that smells of dirty

socks. We hurl through the darkness listening to NPR.
I don't ask what's wrong. Or if everything's okay. I
don't fill the car with chatter. I know that everything is
both okay and not okay.

A quick perusal of my e-mail: twelve publicity pitches
have come in overnight. These have subject lines
such as *Interview Opportunity!* or *Following Up!* The
exclamation point is the new period. Everyone is
always circling back, reaching out, checking in. There
are notes about travel plans, teaching gigs, a fellowship
competition I'm judging. There are notes from Jacob's
school, from his upcoming tennis camp. I just move
down the list and respond to each one with no sense of
priority or order.

My childhood best friend's mom has sent a photo
attachment. *I was driving by the old neighborhood and
thought you'd get a kick out of this.* A redbrick house
with white columns fills the screen. The second-floor
window on the left was my bedroom. The girl who
grew up behind the closed door of that room, madly
scribbling in her journals, looking for some way
out—she left that house and its contents behind like
a discarded chrysalis. I stare at the photo for a long
moment, trying to see inside.

Another e-mail: a $600 bill for a decade of semen
storage from a fertility clinic M. and I visited during a
long-ago attempt to have a second child. I forward it
to M., who is downstairs working. *Did we intend to*

store your semen? A reply comes back a second or two later. *God, no.* An instance in which an exclamation point would be justified.

I know better than to start my day in this manner. What am I supposed to do with these tiny time bombs as they wedge themselves invisibly inside me, ticking, ticking? My childhood home. My husband's frozen semen. I imagine today's missives lining up on some interior shelf. They join all the others, waiting to be understood. At times, the sheer accumulation threatens to overwhelm me. I delete the e-mails or move them into folders. But they hardly disappear.

Jacob laughs when he sees *ex-spouse* under M.'s picture. I tell him we've tried to fix this and have given up. It seems some indifferent algorithm has determined the fate of our marriage. M.'s theory is that my previous marriages must have morphed somehow and created this information. Or misinformation. We can't get rid of it. It relieves me that Jacob isn't perturbed—to the contrary, he thinks it's funny.

Lately, a number of our friends have split up. Families he has grown up with have fractured. The first time it happened, I worried about how to break the news to him.

"I have some sad news," I told him as we drove along a dirt road not far from home. "The ———s are getting a divorce."

He was stunned to hear it—the couple outwardly

made a pretty picture—and asked what would happen next, what it would mean for the kids, to whom he was close.

"I guess they're figuring it out. They'll do what's best for the kids," I answered, then rushed on: "You know everything's okay with Dad and me." Hands on the wheel, eyes on the road. "You know we're always going to be together."

"Of course," he said. "You guys are a power couple."

I looked over at him, surprised. "Yeah, right."

"You are! Like Frank and Claire Underwood from *House of Cards*. Except you're not killing anybody."

I think about what Jacob sees—the public and the private. M. and me at readings, screenings, conferences. M. and me, each of our office doors closed, trying like hell to make a single scene, one sentence, come right. He's seen whole days in which we haven't moved from our chairs. He's seen us fight more than once—both of us red-faced, ugly, our claws out like animals. He's seen tears course down my cheeks. Once, M. threw a dish, then slammed his fist into the wall. Sometimes he'll ask M. how a particular project is going. *It's going*, M. will answer. He's seen us hugging. *Come on, stop it, guys.* In our guest bathroom, framed movie posters, newspaper articles, magazine covers—images of our most burnished selves.

Now he types a note into the app on his phone.

I want to assure you, he writes, *that my parents are very much together.*

The pharmaceutical company has an office in New York, where its creative department is housed on the twelfth floor of a warehouse building. The offices seem dreamt up by a set designer: a vast, open floor plan of workstations at which hives of young men wearing thick black glasses, women with asymmetrical hair sit in front of large video screens. A standard poodle—the pet of the boss—bounds across the floor, or sleeps nestled up against a wall-sized collage dotted with impeccable miniature versions of the company's most famous products.

At meetings with the boss and her team—*team* being a word we have come to use—M. and I sit around a shiny, oval conference table and discuss concept and workflow. We nod and take notes as the boss shares reams of research with us, charts full of arrows and bubbles based on thousands of pages of interviews in the field. Empathy, it seems, can be graphed.

M. does most of the work on the play we produce, approaching this project with the same intensity and focus he brings to his own screenplays. Besides, it's personal. He hardly needs the charts full of arrows.

We hire neighbors of ours—a husband and wife with a long list of Broadway and movie credits—and

turn our library into a makeshift film studio, shelves of
books covered with a backdrop of black cloth held up
by masking tape. The company sends an executive
to our house to supervise the shooting of the video,
a preliminary step for in-house use. They want to
be sure we know what we're doing—and who could
blame them?

But M. does know what he's doing. He's taken the
lead on this project—something he knows he can start
and finish without drama or heartbreak. As M. directs
the video, I stand off to the side with my clipboard,
our script in hand. I give the actors notes, scribble
small revisions. But all the while, a gauzy sense of
unreality hovers. I wonder if our lives have swerved
off course when I wasn't looking. What the hell is
going on? What are these people doing in our house?

I shuffle through the images the pharmaceutical
company plans to project behind the actors during the
live event. Magnified neurons from the somatosensory
cortex float, green and purple, like something out
of a Jackson Pollock painting. Neurons from the
hippocampus spread out like a field of wildflowers.
Beta-amyloid plaques gleam like stars in a twilight sky.
All shockingly beautiful. "This is how it goes," one of
the actors is mid-monologue. "He acts like everything
is okay, and his wife pretends the act is fooling her.
I don't think there's any way to prepare a family for
what this is ultimately like."

· ·

In July of 1939, Virginia Woolf was thinking, as she often did, about time: "The past only comes back when the present runs so smoothly that it is like the sliding surface of a deep river. Then one sees through the surface to the depths . . . But to feel the present sliding over the depths of the past, peace is necessary. The present must be smooth, habitual. For this reason—that it destroys the fullness of life— any break . . . causes me extreme distress; it breaks; it shallows; it turns the depth into hard thin splinters. As I say to L[eonard]: 'What's there real about this? Shall we ever live a real life again?' "

Once a week, sometimes more, I make the two-hour trip into New York City. The city still feels like mine. It hasn't yet churned past me in a blur of cranes, construction, new traffic patterns, whole neighbor-hoods springing up from abandoned train tracks, navy yards, and railway beds. Wherever I go—in every neighborhood—I catch younger versions of myself disappearing around corners.

I emerge from the subway on Seventy-Second and Broadway, a hot breeze blows my hair back, and suddenly my father is holding my hand as we cross the busy street on our way to visit my grandmother on a Sunday afternoon. I stop at a juice bar for a smoothie. It was once a shoe repair shop where I failed to claim a pair of brown suede boots. I buy a *Times* at a newsstand beneath what had been a dance studio in Chelsea, and here I am, at twenty-two, climbing the narrow steps. I am part of a parade of women carrying our gym bags, changing in the cramped bathroom into leotards and leg warmers. Pinning up our hair. Comparing our taut bodies, finding fault with ourselves in the mirror. Some are probably grandmothers by now.

Oh, child! Somewhere inside you, your future has already unfurled like one of those coiled-up party streamers, once shiny, shaken loose, floating gracefully for a brief moment, now trampled underfoot after the party is over. The future you're capable of imagining is already a thing of the past. Who did you think you would grow up to become? You could never have dreamt yourself up. Sit down. Let me tell you everything that's happened. You can stop running now. You are alive in the woman who watches as you vanish.

Each fork in the road: the choice to stay home, to go out, to catch the flight, or cancel it, to take the 1 train, to stop at the bar on the corner. The chance encounters, split-second decisions that make the design—that *are* the design. "For it *is,* always *is,* however we may say it was," wrote Thomas Mann. Back home, I search through my shelf of journals until I find the first one: a tattered red-cloth-covered book decorated with little white flowers. I am sixteen, seventeen, eighteen. I begin to page through it, skimming, really, afraid to look too closely at the words I wrote long ago.

The journal is filled with a stream of endless boys. Names upon names: Neil, Alex, Scott, Eddie, Gil, Dan, Matt. Who were they? Who was I? I was a girl—I had always thought—who believed that men would save me. But perhaps it was darker than that. Perhaps it wasn't being saved that I was after.

The restaurants, street corners, synagogues, university classrooms, distant cities, coffee shops, phone booths, pressurized cabins high above the turning earth. The marriages. *Marriages!* The stories—both the ones that happened and the ones that didn't. The ones eternally bound into the spines of books. The ones that I have polished until they gleam like jewels—until I can say *this is it, precisely it*—that is, until they change on me once more. And then, the ones that are not yet stories: loose fragments within me, sharp as fishhooks. They impale me when I least expect it.

M. knocks on my office door. I'm on my chaise, journals spread all over the floor, trying to gather my whole lost tribe of selves around me.

"What are you doing, honey?" His voice is gentle.

I hold up the tattered red one. It's only by the way he looks at me that I realize my face is streaked with tears.

He sits on my desk chair and swivels toward me.

"This is why I burned every journal I kept from when I was that age," he says. "I didn't want to remember."

I attempt to offer him proof of my fucked-up girlhood in the form of a few choice sentences—but as I read them, I realize they could have been written by any pained, precocious teenager who can't possibly imagine the woman she will become: *I want nobody, I want everybody. I want a stable man in my life. One who will be there, but will give me enough room to be free, to breathe, to live. And one I can love, but not sacrifice my soul for.*

I cannot bring myself to even idly wish any of it—not even the most painful parts—away. *Eighteen years.* Change even one moment, and the whole thing unravels. The narrative thread doesn't stretch in a line from end to end, but rather, spools and unspools, loops around and returns again and again to the same spot.

Come closer now and listen. Be thankful for all of it. You would not have walked into that Gramercy Park apartment. You would not have looked into the eyes of the war correspondent just back from Mogadishu. A *coup de foudre:* a bolt of lightning. You would not have your bright and sunny boy. There is no other life than this. You would not have stumbled into the vastly imperfect, beautiful, impossible present.

"Be who you needed when you were younger," someone called Momastery posts on Instagram.

· ·

In an extraordinary photographic series, *Imagine Finding Me,* the Tokyo-born, London-based photographer Chino Otsuka uses digital technology to insert images of her adult self into existing images of herself as a girl in the 1970s and '80s. Here she is— a grown woman in a dark peasant blouse and denim skirt—walking beside a solemn child of perhaps five or six, on a windswept beach in Kamakura, Japan. Their shadows glisten behind them in the smooth wet sand. And here they are again, the two of them, sharing a park bench in the Jardin du Luxembourg, facing in opposite directions. Now the girl has made a dirty snowman. She stares unsmilingly at the camera in her striped socks, one hand draped protectively over its melting shape. Her future self stands nearby in a fur-lined parka.

All the woman can do is hover like something spectral, otherworldly. The sense is that she's watching over the girl from a benign distance. She passes by her on a staircase to a Buddhist temple. In a Tokyo train station, she stands behind her and appears to be carrying her bags. Otsuka's technical skills are such that no doubt she could have allowed the woman to reach out and rest a hand on the girl's small shoulder, as if to say: *Don't worry, I'm here.* But in none of the ten photographs do they ever touch.

· ·

Sometimes M.'s father is charming—a flirtatious, funny, generous character—but other times a darkness emerges from a coiled place within him, as sudden and vicious as a rattlesnake. All his children adore him, but they also know that he can turn on just about anyone. The worst I've seen him is when he lashes out at M.—his firstborn son, the one who left.

A few winters ago, M. set out to make his own movie. As he wrote the script, which he planned to direct himself, I watched his disappointment fall away in layers. Over the course of an intense, high-risk year, he raised the money. It was the same year his hair went completely white. He found his way into the offices of some big Hollywood agents and had actors vying for the starring role. He wasn't playing by the rules—in fact, there was no rule book. The actors were cast believing the money was there. The investors came on board assured that the actors were cast. The clock was ticking. Every day was dangerous. This renegade, rogue approach seemed to serve and feed him. He was alive—in combat mode—bristling with energy.

Finally, finally.

The heart of the film—my favorite part—centered on the long marriage of an elderly couple, a slightly kinder, gentler version of my in-laws. It was a son's love letter, a darkly comic paean to his parents. As M.

was making the film, I prayed his father would live long enough to see it.

Just before the film was to open in New York, the whole family was together—about to go out to dinner for my in-laws' anniversary—when M. pulled a DVD out of his briefcase and suggested showing a scene or two. It's always loud in my in-laws' house—even when they're the only ones there, the television blares at full volume—but at that moment it was quiet enough to hear M.'s father's voice rise above all the others.

"I don't fucking want to see that piece of crap," he said.

I watched M.'s face slacken and absorb the blow.

"Your mother's furious about it," my father-in-law went on.

My mother-in-law sat there staring into space, not looking furious about anything.

"What are you talking about?" M. asked.

"You show her no respect—I've read interviews. You make fun of her Alzheimer's."

The cousins—ranging from ages ten to twenty—looked back and forth between M. and his father.

"I do no such thing, Dad."

"I don't give a shit."

"You haven't even seen it."

"Yeah, and I'm not going to."

Nobody said another word as we left the house and got into our car—the three of us—presumably to caravan to the restaurant. M. started the engine but didn't move. He was doing that rapid-blinking thing. We sat there in the darkness of his parents' driveway.

From Carl Jung: "Until you make the unconscious conscious, it will direct your life, and you will call it fate."

A photo of M. has surfaced on a private Facebook page for a group of journalists who had covered the famine and conflict in Somalia in the 1990s. The page—called The Sahafi Rooftop Club—is named after the hotel where all the journalists stayed when in Mogadishu. There are thirty-eight members in the closed group. Many of the photos are of their dead colleagues. Carlos Mavroleon, who died in Peshawar, Pakistan, while preparing to cross the border into Afghanistan to find and interview Osama Bin Laden. Dan Eldon, Hansi Kraus, Anthony Macharia, and Hos Maina, who were stoned and beaten to death by a mob on the streets of Mogadishu.

In the photo, M. sits cross-legged on the tile floor of a dim hallway at the Sahafi. The year is 1993, three years before we met. With him are the Nairobi correspondent for *The New York Times*, a reporter for CBS, and a few Somali assistants and fixers. M. is

smoking a cigarette, as he is in just about every image
I've seen of him from that time. He's tanned, his hair
is long, and he's skinnier than I've ever known him to
be. Notably, he is the only journalist in the photograph
not wearing a flak jacket.

They had gathered in an interior corridor because
there was heavy gunfire on the streets. High-
powered bullets will rip through concrete blocks.
One morning M. woke up in his room at the Sahafi,
the usual pitch-black bisected by a bright beam of
light streaming through a bullet hole in the wall near
his bed. So why wasn't he wearing a flak jacket?
He looks exposed and vulnerable next to the other
journalists who are protected by forty pounds of
body armor.

"The people who worked for the major news
outlets had to wear them. No one at *The Village
Voice* gave a shit," M. tells me as we scroll down the
page for The Sahafi Rooftop Club, past image
after image of handsome, dead young men.
"I had one, but I didn't like it," he says. "I wore
it for my first three or four days and never
again."

I return to the photo of M. and his colleagues and
examine my future husband's face. He knew how to
move like an alley cat through the streets of a war
zone in which ambushes, kidnappings, car crashes, and
stray bullets were to be expected. The more dangerous
the situation, the slower his pulse. In the photo he

looks relaxed—strangely at peace, at home in a world in which he was unprotected and bullets were flying.

On a promotional video for a skin-tightening ultrasound procedure called Ultherapy on a cosmetic dermatologist's website—the kind of thing a web-surfing, middle-aged writer might find herself exploring on a rough morning—a clay model of a woman's head commands my attention. The caption reads: *Face Aging—30 Years.*

One click and electronic music with a heavy beat—think Moscow nightclub—begins to blast from my laptop. The clay woman's head fills the screen. *The Young Face.* We contemplate the lovely planes of her cheeks, her high, smooth forehead—she looks to be in her twenties—when suddenly two hands wielding a sculptor's modeling tool enter the picture and begin working on her face, which, it turns out, is made not of dry but of soft, wet clay, and is subject to revision.

The film speeds up, the music pounds, the hands with the tool move at a dizzying pace, faster than the eye can track. Her cheeks are slightly flattened, lines etched into her forehead, her neck softened. We now share another long moment with her more weathered self. She appears to be a person who has lived awhile. She has a few wrinkles around her eyes and looks like she could use a nap. *Early Changes.*

Just as we are getting used to these changes, the

music kicks up a notch—the sound is like the loud, sped-up ticking of a clock—and back come the hands at warp speed, and the modeling tool, now carving deeper lines, moving faster and more carelessly, extending the tip of her nose, tugging beneath her eyes, pulling down her earlobes, pinching under her chin. When the hands are finished, she is slowly rotated back so she is directly facing the viewer. Now she's an old woman. *Later changes.*

The sculptor's strong, fine hands have completed their work. The final moments of the video are in triptych form. We see all three faces close-up—I can't stop looking at the one in the middle—as the music continues its ceaseless beat.

Breakfast arrived on a tray—fresh fruit, yogurt, croissants, etc. We decided to explore a bit, aided by Hector (the owner) and his maps. We drove to Vaison-la-Romaine and then on to Crestet—a tiny, magnificent town perched on the top of a hill. We parked and walked to the top. There was a little café —Le Panorama—where we had lunch. Then we got lost. We went back to Crillon le Brave. That night we went to Le Bontoy for dinner outdoors next to their swimming pool. A great country dinner. M. had incredible langoustine. Went back to Crillon for dessert and café overlooking the hills of Provence.

· ·

M. and I go see a couples therapist. *Eighteen years.*
Things come up in the course of eighteen years.
Together we've weathered Jacob's illness, my
mother's death, his mother's decline. We've fought
each other's battles: my bad reviews feel even worse
to M. than they do to me. A friend's betrayal of him
makes me want to come out swinging. We're each
other's first readers. We have always been on the
same side. When people ask if we're competitive
with one another—two writers under the same roof—
the question itself seems absurd. We're *together*. All in.
Deep inside the us of us.

So why—the therapist wonders—are we here?

M. sits silently, so I begin.

"I'm frightened," I say. And then I start to cry.

I feel M. next to me on her sofa. His body is
my home. Yet lately, I have had flashes, unbidden
moments in which I wonder who the hell he is. I
secretly fear that I've been wrong about him.

While M. was making the movie, he let things slide.
Bills piled up. I trusted he knew what he was doing.
Then our Writers Guild health insurance lapsed, and
he didn't tell me. Ever since I found out, I've been in
a panic. It feels like every step I take is fraught with
danger. As if the earth's crust might just open up and
swallow me whole. What if something happened to
one of us? Just yesterday I didn't let Jacob go out for
a bike ride. I was afraid he'd fall and break his leg.

I'll take care of it.

M.'s head is in his hands. He knows just how badly he's fucked up. His voice is low, muted.

"I'm sorry," he says.

I'm not interested in sorry.

"I didn't want to disappoint you. I just wanted to fix things."

My voice, too, sounds different to my ears. Reedy, shaking with rage.

"You put our family in danger," I say.

"What are you most afraid of?" the therapist asks.

Just a short while earlier, as we walked to our appointment on West Ninth Street—a pretty block just off Fifth Avenue—I had noticed an elderly homeless woman pushing a cart filled with all her worldly belongings. Who had she been? How had she gotten there? It seemed a possibility that I could become that elderly homeless woman someday. That this life M. and I have built together is flimsy, the world merciless, and time, time unrelenting.

I see M. in my peripheral vision as I stutter out my worst fears. He flinches at my mention of the homeless woman. The therapist tilts her head to one side. She hardly knows me and has no reason to believe what sounds like histrionics of the creative class. *Really? That's what you're most afraid of?* As if it were ridiculous. As if it were simply out of the realm of possibility.

· ·

Late summer. At our local farmer's market, I wait in
line for goat's milk yogurt, green roses, sourdough
bread, fresh eggs while M. picks up some beef to grill.
It's a bright, sunny day—with just a hint of autumn
in the air—but I'm not feeling bright or sunny. It has
been a difficult stretch. I usually find the ritual of the
farmer's market cheering, but today it is as if a pane
of glass separates me from the crowds of tanned,
fit shoppers carrying their eco-friendly mesh bags.
*Well, you've had a great summer. Seems like you've been
everywhere!*

A woman we used to know stops me to ask if it was
M. she just saw—"I thought it was him but nearly
didn't recognize him with that big white beard." Does
M. have a big white beard? I don't think so. When I
find him on the other side of the market, I look at him
the way an outsider might. His hair is wild. His shirt
untucked, the hems of his jeans frayed. *Get a grip!*
I think, but don't say. *You look like the Unabomber!*
It's true. He hasn't shaved in days.

We've been working all morning—Jacob had a
sleepover and we're taking advantage of our empty
house—each of us hunched over our laptops. M. is
putting the finishing touches on a television pilot about
which he has once again mustered high hopes. I've
been on social media promoting an upcoming writing
workshop. I post a photo of myself seated in lotus
position on a small platform, in deep conversation
with a student. And another: a panoramic view of the

Berkshires. *Come join me for an inspirational, generative retreat!* I am not feeling like someone who knows how to inspire anyone or generate anything.

I stop into the bookstore before we head home. I've been searching for a particular poem Richard Wilbur wrote about his wife. I scan the *W*s, but there is no Richard Wilbur. In its place is a mis-shelved slim volume called *The Country of Marriage*. Again, Wendell Berry.

In the car—waiting for M. to pick up our dry cleaning—I turn to the title poem: "Sometimes our life reminds me / of a forest in which there is a graceful clearing / and in that opening a house, / an orchard and a garden, / comfortable shades, and flowers / red and yellow in the sun, a pattern / made in the light for the light to return to. / The forest is mostly dark, its ways / to be made anew day after day, the dark / richer than the light and more blessed / provided we stay brave / enough to keep on going in."

Our first date: M. picks me up at my apartment on a blustery Friday afternoon in early November. The plan is to take a walk—perhaps stop into a museum or two—and end up downtown for dinner. He's made a reservation at a small, dark Italian place in the East Village, near where he lives.

I invite him in. In the week since we met at the

Halloween party, I have wondered if the powerful magic between us might have been a figment, a cruel illusion—but as soon as our eyes meet, there it is, unmistakable. It winds its way around us, pulling us together. We're all over my apartment—in the wing chair in my office, the sofa in the living room—our hands, our mouths, ravenous. It isn't just desire—though there's plenty of that—but something else underneath. A sense of recognition. A sense of inevitability. It will turn out that we won't leave each other's sides all weekend long—or practically ever again.

We head out into the brisk afternoon. We're walking down Broadway when M. tells me he needs to make a quick stop way west on Fifty-Seventh Street—the studios for CBS News. M.'s last trip to Somalia had been for *60 Minutes*—as one of the only American journalists who knew the territory, he had been hired to help produce a piece for Christiane Amanpour—and now that he is back home, he needs to pick up his paycheck.

An envelope has been left for him at the reception desk. Beneath the watchful portraits of Morley Safer and Lesley Stahl, he stuffs it into the back pocket of his jeans. I don't stop to wonder about any of this. It makes perfect sense. The check is large, and it can't wait the weekend. He's been out of the country for a month. His bills are overdue. It's important that he deposit the check into his account before the end of the business day.

Back on the street, we find a nearby Citibank.
He removes the check from the envelope, endorses
it, and inserts it into the ATM. If he's nervous—or
relieved—at the close call, I am unaware of it. None
of this seems precarious to me. It's the most natural
thing, part of the job.

*And that it may be true, at least in poetic terms, that
beginnings are like seeds that contain within them
everything that will ever happen.*

We walk—arms wrapped around each other—
downtown. The romantic dinner, candles dripping,
his East Village apartment, the two of us tangled up
in his bedsheets. The tiny wedding; the Provençal
honeymoon; the birth of our baby; the close call. The
raising of him, the reveling in him. The Brooklyn
town house, the Connecticut saltbox. The lung cancer,
the Alzheimer's. The bar mitzvah. The triumphs;
disappointments; terrors; risks. The books; films;
teaching; travel. The smart moves; the idiocy. The
sheer velocity of it all. I want to bless that young
couple as they cross Union Square. I want to deliver
some kind of benediction upon them as—drunk on
love—they meander the narrow streets of Alphabet
City. I want to suggest that there will come a time
when they will need something more than love.

· ·

On the Valentine's Day 1998 episode of *This American Life,* Ira Glass interviews Cornell Professor Emeritus of French Literature Richard Klein. They've been discussing Dante and Beatrice, Petrarch and Laura. In the thirteenth century, Petrarch encountered Laura as he walked by a fountain in the south of France. He looked into her eyes, and in that instant, his life was transformed. He wrote the first lyric love poem ever written.

But eventually the conversation takes a semi-depressing turn: "Psychologists have estimated that you can only stay in love for eighteen months," says Klein. "That's the limit. After that it becomes admiration, respect, affection, but—"

And here Ira Glass interrupts him: "The dream of it dissolves and it becomes something else."

For nearly two decades I have become almost synonymous with M. I can hardly attend a party or gathering solo without the question being asked: *Where's M.?* We have formed ourselves over the years as two branches form, twisting, rooting, growing, stunting, pushing, budding, stagnating, reaching ever farther, together. Who would I have become without him?

Until M., I was good at leaving. *If you find yourself in the wrong story, leave*—a piece of online folk wisdom. I wasn't so skilled at avoiding getting into the wrong story to begin with—but once there, I knew how to extricate myself. Houdini-like, I would test myself to see just how far I could go. With hands and feet bound together, I would slither and slip my way out of mess after tangled mess.

One rainy afternoon, an invitation to a high school reunion leads me to the discovery that my first boyfriend is the math coordinator at a prep school less than a half-hour from my house. Surprisingly little information is available about him beyond this fact. I peer at the stamp-sized photo on the school's website, searching for the boy in the man. I close my eyes and inhale the scent of damp earth, the mossy bark of trees in the woods where we hung out when we cut school. The sounds of a basketball game—bank shot echoing through the gym. A long shrill whistle. He has no Facebook page, no LinkedIn profile. This makes me wonder whether he's isolated and unhappy, though it may signify the opposite. I can't tell if he's married or has kids. I hope he does. I wonder if he's ever looked me up—I am nothing if not visible online.

Without moving from my spot on the chaise in my office, I embark on a virtual tour of my romantic history. My first husband lives in New Orleans with his wife and young daughter. He runs a World Music record label. No surprises here. I knew all this before running into him in the corridor of the Mark Twain Museum. There is a kind and gentle light in his eyes. I'll bet he's a good family man.

The toxic married boyfriend with whom I spent my early twenties is recently dead. His face peers out from an obituary notice that fills my screen. Dead! He died just around the time I began writing this book. A few swift clicks lead me to the discovery that he split with his wife—the one he cheated on with me—and married a much younger woman with whom he has a boy around Jacob's age.

I look up my second husband. He's a financial adviser in New York City and is married—but leaves virtually no digital footprint. It takes effort to lead such an untraceable life. I find him only because his stepdaughter is a prima ballerina. I do manage to figure out that he and his wife live in a very nice Park Avenue building. Judging from his campaign contributions, he continues to be a Democrat. I can discern nothing in the way of his happiness, his level of contentment. Did I leave a trace on him? Did he leave one on me? This man once told me he had never made a mistake in his life. *You're looking at her,* I thought at the time.

There are various flings. *Keith, Gary, William.* I certainly remember them better than the names scrawled in my red cloth journal, names from the years that seem to seesaw backward. The actor now sells residential real estate in South Africa. The television writer is listed on Wikipedia as a folk artist. The photographer is still a photographer.

In the jumble of memory, I see flashbulbs. A New

Year's Eve dinner around a table in Southampton;
a late-night motorcycle ride down a dark stretch of
lower Broadway; being backed against a wall for a first
kiss. Near the end of Delmore Schwartz's "In Dreams
Begin Responsibilities," a minor character turns to the
twenty-one-year-old narrator of the story and chides
him: "You can't carry on like this, it is not right, you
will find that out soon enough, everything you do
matters too much."

The years. They ran through my open fingers like
a trickle of water, streaming faster, faster. On my
twenty-fifth birthday, I wept in the outdoor garden of
a café on West Seventy-First Street that no longer
exists. I was sure my best years were behind me. At
thirty, my second husband threw me a party in our
apartment high above Madison Avenue. I wore a
blue sparkly minidress. I left him two months later.
At thirty-four, I walked into the crowded party near
Gramercy Park. At thirty-seven, I gave birth by
emergency cesarean section. At thirty-nine, I left New
York City. At forty, my mother died. And then a long,
merciful stretch of ordinary days. What will be next
on the list? There has always been more time.

The woodpecker has returned. I see him as I get out
of the shower. He's latched onto the gutter, his small

head hammering away at the very siding we had replaced months ago.

"Honey!" I call from the top of the stairs.

No response from down below. M. has lived with a high-pitched ringing in his ears ever since a Hot Tuna concert in 1975. Lately it seems to have grown worse.

I walk halfway down the stairs and call again. As I'm toweling off, I hear his footsteps. I know those footsteps well. The slow, plodding ones when he's tired. The staccato ones when he has some sort of news. These contain a measure of apprehension. *What now?*

Together, we watch as the bird pecks away at a small hole in the siding.

"I can't believe he's back," I say.

"It's probably not the same one."

"Oh, it's the same one."

"How do you know?"

"I just do."

M. has given up on the pellet gun. He probably wishes he had his Kalashnikov. *Nail* the fucker. But by now I know that we're in a dance with the woodpecker that will continue as the seasons turn. We can't catch him, and he's not going away. He'll hammer his holes into our house. We'll patch the holes, or replace the siding, repaint, depending on what's called for, and what we can afford. And then he'll hammer them again.

· ·

M.'s manager reads the new television pilot he's been working on for the past six months—a subtle, dark comedy—and suggests that it would benefit from "more noise." M. is not sure what "more noise" means. The manager proposes adding a transsexual to the mix. This news comes the same week that the shooting schedule for M.'s next film is postponed because a) the money hasn't been raised, b) the female lead hasn't been cast, and c) the famous comedian attached to the project will now not be available until next year.

What next? What next?

I pore over online listings for academic teaching jobs. It has been years since I've taught in universities. Instead, I've created a life in which I teach in far-flung places—Taos, Aspen, Provincetown, Stockbridge, Positano—which often double as vacations for my family. It's a lovely life. You might even say it's a work of art. But in the middle of the night, when the ticking clock, the snoring husband, the restless dogs become cacophonous, my mind tilts and whirls as old terrors take on new forms.

"_____ is advertising a position for a distinguished writer in residence," I say to M. "And _____ is looking for a full professor. Then there's _____, which is for only one year, but I've heard there's a possibility they may extend it into a permanent position."

"Is that what you want?" M. asks.

"Is that what I *want*?"

We stare at each other across the kitchen table.
Morning light filters though the leaves of the old
Japanese tree out back, creating a strobe effect. I think
of one of my dearest friends, a Buddhist teacher in her
late seventies—contentedly married for sixty years—
and a favorite mantra of hers: *It isn't what I wanted.
But it's what I've got.*

"I'm just thinking about the long run," I say to
M. after a beat. I need to choose my words carefully.
When we finish this conversation, he will go back
into his office and begin the work of unraveling
his meticulously written television pilot in order to
provide more "noise." The process is a bit like taking
apart the inner workings of a well-made Swiss watch
and spreading the pieces all over the table until they
become something else entirely, something that
perhaps no longer tells time.

"You know. Things like pensions, health insurance.
We can't keep living this way forever."

M. takes a long sip from his mug of coffee. It
displays a whimsical, hand-drawn mermaid—one
of Odysseus's sirens—the symbol of the writers'
conference we started in Italy ten years ago. We made
the conference. We made the mug. We made this life.

"Everything will be fine in the long run," M. says.
"We just have an immediate problem. I have to fix
this fucking script. That's what's right in front of me.
Today. If I think about the future—"

"But somebody has to think about the future,"
I blurt out.

I've now entered dangerous territory. Our morning is in jeopardy. Our days require our minds to be clear, unconfused, free of anxiety or anger.

"Let's not do this now," I say. I scrape my chair back, startling one of the dogs. "Let's just get to work."

"The constitutional disease from which I suffer," wrote the philosopher and psychologist William James, "is what the Germans call *Zerrissenheit*, or torn-to-pieces-hood. The days are broken in pure zig-zag and interruption."

Lately I've been hearing a whispered admonition in my ear as I go about my business. Or perhaps admonition isn't quite right. It seems more of a quiet, urgent instruction issued from a place in the deep interior that holds within it everything I still need to know: dense matter, a dark star.

Be careful, the voice says.

I'm walking down Madison Avenue with a friend on a beautiful spring afternoon when my stupid platform shoe hits a divot in the pavement, and I go down hard—the flat of one hand, a knee, my cheekbone slam into the asphalt. *Oh my god, are you okay?* I don't stop moving, even though I'm not at all sure I'm okay. I stand up again and limp to the corner to assess the damage. My knee is bloody. My hand is scraped.

My cheekbone stings. But it's the feeling, more than anything—I am flooded with a sense of frailty and shame. How could this have happened to me? How could I have tripped so clumsily? And most of all: How could I have gone down so fast? The whole episode took an instant. A heartbeat.

Be careful, the voice says.

I meet another friend for a glass of wine at our local watering hole that turns into two, maybe even two and a half glasses. Driving home, I notice a car trailing me. The country roads are quiet. The way to my house is meandering. The car is still behind me at a safe distance, twin beams of headlights in my rear-view mirror. Did someone follow me home from the bar? The paranoid thought makes me grip the wheel harder. Or wait: Is it a cop? I drive carefully, and my breath returns to my body only after I've pulled into my driveway and the car continues on. There are so many ways a life can get messed up. So many wrong turns from which it is difficult to recover.

Be careful, the voice says.

A man flirts with me at a party. From time to time, a business card offered, pressed into my hand. A cocked eyebrow. A sweeping glance. A suggestive e-mail. An invitation. The husband of a friend. A writer at a conference. It has been easy to shut down even a whiff of an offer. But then there are the ones—I'm sure M. has them, too—who would have caught my interest in another life. Around these men I am even more cautious. I wouldn't want anyone to get the wrong idea. *Eighteen years.*

The stumbles and falls; the lapses in judgment; the near misses; the could-haves. I've become convinced that our lives are shaped less by the mistakes we make than when we make them. There is less elasticity now. Less time to bounce back. And so I heed the urgent whisper and move with greater and greater deliberation. I hold my life with M. carefully in my hands like the faience pottery we brought back from our honeymoon long ago. We are delicate. We are beautiful. We are not new. We must be handled with care.

I used to tell my students that in order to write memoir—or at least *good* memoir, the kind that will be of value to the disinterested reader—the writer has to have some distance from the material. I was quite certain that we could not write directly from our feelings, but only the memory of our feelings. How else to find the necessary ironic distance, the cool remove? How else to shape a narrative but from the insight and wisdom of retrospect?

But like every fixed idea, this one has lost its hold on me as years have passed and the onrushing present—the only place from which the writer can tell the story—continues to shift along with the sands of time. Our recollections alter as we attempt to gather

them. Even retrospect is mutable. Perspective, a
momentary figment of consciousness. Memoir freezes
a moment like an insect trapped in amber. Me now, me
then. This woman, that girl. It all keeps changing. And
so: If retrospect is an illusion, then why not attempt
to tell the story as I'm inside of it? Which is to say:
before the story has become a story?

A few years after we moved to Connecticut, we awoke
early one autumn morning to a world blanketed in
snow. A freak storm had descended upon us overnight.
The ground was not yet frozen, and the weight
of the heavy, wet snow on leaf-covered branches
pulled whole root systems from the soft earth. Bits
of russet and golden yellow could be seen here and
there, remnants of a dead season. In the quiet of our
meadow, we stood still, listening to the sound of the
splitting, cracking, toppling forest in the distance.

We lost power, of course, and we had no generator.
Trees had crashed into power lines all over the county,
making many roads impassable. We had no heat, no
water, since our well is operated by an electric pump.
Using the little battery power we had left on our cell
phones, we called friends who had a guesthouse with
a generator and made the decision to try to make our
way over there.

"I've driven in worse," M. said as he maneuvered
our four-wheel-drive truck down our long driveway,

making fresh tracks in drifts that were several feet high. Jacob was strapped into the backseat. Our new puppy whined in his crate.

The driveway narrowed and suddenly tree branches were directly in front of our windshield.

"Shit."

Jacob started to laugh.

"Fuck."

We sat there for a moment, motor idling. There was no going forward and no going back. My mind raced with what to do. Before we left the house, M. had tossed his chainsaw into the way back of the truck. The chainsaw—one of his earliest purchases when we first moved to the country—was a bone of contention. I saw it not as a useful power tool, but rather as an instrument of potential carnage. In a flash I imagined M. losing control of the thing—blood seeping into snow.

"I'm going to take a look."

"No!" I put a hand on his arm.

If we had to, we could abandon the truck and hike back up to the house. But then what? We could be stranded up there for days.

"Okay. Let's do it this way, then." M. gunned the gas and we crashed through the low-lying branches. We skidded onto the road, the back of the truck shimmying. *I'll take care of it.* An electrical pole hung diagonally above us, resting against some power lines that looked ready to snap. Our neighbor's ancient

apple tree was on its side, its gnarled roots exposed.
The natural world was a cemetery full of pillaged
graves.

We drove in silence. I gripped the sides of the
passenger seat and tried to breathe. What if we slid off
the road and down an embankment? What if no one
found us? I hadn't seen a single other car. What if we
were electrocuted by a power surge from a loose wire?

M. turned onto a street that didn't lead to our
friends' house.

"What are you *doing*?"

"I want to see what's going on. Just get a better
sense of what's out here."

"Could you please just not?"

But M.'s response to crisis had taken over. I could
feel every nerve in him bristling and alive. He fiddled
with the radio dial, listening for the latest report on
the storm. Eyes darting everywhere. We could have
been in Mogadishu. We could have been stopped at
a checkpoint, surrounded by guns. M. once told me
he had always carried a pack of cigarettes when he
was overseas so that he could defuse a situation by
offering one to a jumpy rebel soldier. I pictured him
now, holding out a Marlboro, hands steady. Making a
life-or-death educated guess.

"Turn around," I said.

"Wait, let's just go a little—"

"Turn the fuck around." My voice was shaking.

He glanced at me and did as I asked. Felled frozen

branches ground under our wheels. The radio crackled
with warnings from the governor, pleas from law
enforcement to stay off the roads, stories of terrible
accidents and stranded motorists. I swiveled to look
at Jacob, who had fallen asleep in his booster seat: his
blond curls, eyelashes dark against his soft cheeks.
Didn't M. know me? This kind of danger set off in me
an avalanche of old terrors.

That afternoon—Jacob and I ensconced in the
warmth of our friends' guesthouse—M. headed
back out into the tundra. Armed with his chainsaw,
he rescued a family whose car was wedged beneath
a fallen tree. He cleared a path so an elderly woman
could take refuge in a nearby home. He made turns
down blocked roads with no one to tell him to *please
stop, don't do it, it's too dangerous*. He sidestepped
electrical wires and spoke with emergency crews.
When he returned to the guesthouse, he was ex-
hilarated, his cheeks ruddy, eyes bright. I hated him.

"It's like a war zone out there," he said.

During rush-hour traffic, I hear an advertisement on
the radio for something called letsmakeaplan.org.
A worried-sounding male voice asks the listener:
Are you prepared for major life events? Have you
considered your retirement goals? Alone in the car, I
contemplate my answer. When I arrive back home,
I look up the website, which turns out, unsurprisingly,

to be run by an organization of certified financial planners. Amid advice about lifelong financial strategies, steps to financial confidence, and the new financial realities, the title of one particular article catches my eye: *Uncertainty Is Inevitable*. It's a catchy phrase. But I'm not sure it's quite right. *Inevitable* would seem to imply that uncertainty will at some point assert itself. Whereas it seems to me that uncertainty is a permanent condition—in fact, the only thing about which we can be certain.

That night, I lie in bed next to M. in the darkness, his face illuminated by the glow of his iPad as he works on his daily crossword puzzle. His glasses are perched on the tip of his nose. Twenty-five across: Professor Borg in Bergman's *Wild Strawberries*. Fourteen down: Major U.S.-Spanish language daily. When did doing the crossword become part of his routine? If I had to pinpoint it, I'd say it was seven or eight years ago, around the time his mother was diagnosed with Alzheimer's.

In a children's book by Michael Foreman called *Fortunately, Unfortunately,* a young boy named Milo is charged with taking his grandmother's umbrella back to her house. Fortunately, he liked going to Granny's house. Unfortunately, it began to storm. Fortunately, he had the umbrella. Unfortunately, he slipped and fell off a cliff and into the sea. Fortunately, the umbrella acted as a parachute. Unfortunately, there was a whale. Fortunately, inside the whale there was a pirate ship.

Unfortunately, the pirate wasn't a nice guy. And so
forth. This being a children's book, after hurricanes,
volcanoes, dinosaurs, spaceships, and huge aliens,
Milo makes it safely to his grandmother's house with
a dented umbrella (unfortunately) fortunately full of
pirate treasure.

In a life made up of fortune and its flip side, M.
and I have never had a plan. We've made it up as
we've gone along, and for the most part, we've made
it work. But what if it stops working? What if we
run into a wall too high to scale? What if life throws
something at us that we can't solve with the sheer
force of our wits and wills? The great adventures
and unexpected joys have outweighed the sleepless
nights—fortunately. *Happy accidents*, I've called them.
My emphasis—always—on *happy*.

Nearly twenty years ago—at work on my first
memoir—I packed all my journals into a box and
brought them with me to an artists' colony where
I had been granted a fellowship to spend the month
of August. My intention was to reread the journals in
chronological order. My hope was to jog my memory,
or perhaps even capture something of the voice of
my younger self.

That first morning, I climbed upstairs with my
coffee, settled myself at my desk, and opened the
red-cloth-covered journal decorated with the little

white flowers. The rest of the journals were piled
by my side. My room was large and ornate, with
mullioned windows, built-in bookcases, and a fainting
couch upholstered in faded velvet.

My work was cut out for me. I began to read as
the early-morning light crept across the room, dust
motes like translucent pillars in the air. I'm not sure
how far into that first journal I read that morning. The
next thing I knew, it was early afternoon and I was on
the fainting couch. Hours had gone by. The journal
was on the floor. I had entered some sort of fugue
state that came upon me like a sudden fever. The
journals—I understood at once—were dangerous.
If I read further, I might never write the memoir.
I had no sympathy for the girl I once was. She was
boy-crazy, insipid, ridiculous. I was certain she didn't
deserve a book. I didn't want to capture her voice.
I packed the whole lot of them back in the box, taped
it shut, and hauled it down to my car. I pushed her as
far away from me as possible.

But now she's back—she won't leave me alone.
Twenty years. The red-cloth-covered journal has
yielded its tarnished treasures. The next in order—
and the last handwritten one—is improbably large.
An unwieldy square shape with a hard spine, it is
designed by someone named Cinzia Ruggeri and
has an epigraph written in Italian: *Questa agenda e*

l'espressione di una grande ambizione. This journal is the expression of a grand ambition. And indeed, it seems to be. Each page is artfully illustrated: a bird, a spatter of blood, a key, a broken heart. It opens with a line drawing of a Roman column.

> *Hangover to start 1986. Last night, Château Margaux '75 and Cristal at midnight. Like a scene from a Michelob commercial. Why are these things never that way when we are living them? Resolutions? Millions, all boring. Spent the day wondering why I'm depressed, determined that this year will be different.*

That first page of the elaborate Italian diary ends with a quote that I must have meticulously transcribed from the diary of Anaïs Nin: *"Oh how many pleasures, of what a sweet life she has deprived us, I said to myself, by reason of this savage obstinacy to deny her inclination."*

Five weeks after I wrote those words—on a snowy February night—my father passed out at the wheel as he drove with my mother on a wide stretch of New Jersey highway. Their car barreled across the divider into oncoming traffic and made three entire solitary loops before crashing into a concrete embankment. By the time they were pried from the wreckage, both were near death. On the other side of the country— deep in the practice of my savage obstinacy—I slept

through the night as my parents were raced to the
nearest hospital. It was morning before my phone
rang. Twenty-four hours before I was able to get
a flight home in the blizzard. Two weeks before my
father died. It was not the education I wanted, but
it's the one I got.

A student at a weekend workshop gives me a book.
He tells me it practically fell into his hands earlier that
day in a used bookstore in town, and he wanted me to
have it. I leaf through it and discover an underlined
passage: "Rabbi Zusya said, 'In the coming world,
they will not ask me: "Why were you not Moses?"
They will ask me: "Why were you not Zusya?" ' "

In cleaning out my office one afternoon, I discover
a dusty folder that contains M.'s report cards from
grade school through graduate school that my in-laws
must have sent home with us after a visit. Teacher
after teacher expresses profound disappointment, even
anger, at his lack of interest and performance.

M. has been an outsider most of the time in this course.
I'm not sure he's done much of the reading.

M.'s daily work has been very poor. He has frequently
not done his homework.

M.'s writing is not entirely adequate for his age.
Organizing his thoughts to write a story is apparently
quite hard for him.

He is reluctant to express himself both orally and in
writing—but I am hopeful that he will change as he
gets older.

I leaf through the tissue-thin, typewritten reports,
feeling concern for this boy who I don't yet know or
love. I'm afraid to read on, as if I don't know what
will happen next. But then the folder—by his senior
year in college—begins to tell another story:

M. was one of the most intellectually gifted of the
participants in class. He was generous with his
thoughts and put his ideas on the line. M. has writing
ability and a keen sense of humor. He led a discussion
of The Brothers Karamazov *and held fast for the*
best in Ivan Karamazov and the intellect against the
spiritualists and Dostoyevsky.

What happened? And when—and why? Was the
man evident in the child? How did that disaffected
and underdeveloped boy become M.? Perhaps my
future husband was just slumbering, waiting to
be woken up by an explosion. I picture the two of
us—M. and me—each blind to our own potential
selves, a generation and several states, even conti-

nents, apart. Twin messes. Each of us shocked into adulthood.

At the end of the first evening at a large retreat, an old man approaches as I'm packing up my books and papers for the night. He looks at me with such warmth and love. Startled, I glance down at his name tag. I raise a hand to my mouth, then stand and hug him hard, wordlessly. He had been my first piano teacher.

"I read a book review of yours in the *Times*," he tells me. "Which led me to read all of your work. I had to come see you."

I was perhaps in second grade when I first began to take lessons from him. My mother would drive me to his studio, where I would diligently perform my scales and arpeggios as he paced the room. He was a serious pianist and expected commitment from his students. He gave me music before I found words. For a while, I lived to please him. As my abilities grew, I secretly taught myself a Mozart sonata considerably beyond my reach and surprised him one day by sitting at the piano and playing the first movement. The light in his eyes! The sense that I had accomplished something! What year did I stop practicing? Fourteen? Fifteen?

He has traveled hundreds of miles to see me. He tells me of the loss of one of his adult children, tears standing still in his eyes. *What's left?* he wonders aloud. *What's left?* He asks the question as if he believes I may know the answer. At first, I feel a wave of fear. What do I know? What can I possibly offer this man who saved me every Wednesday afternoon of my childhood? "My life has accumulated behind my own back while I was living it, like money in the bank, and I am receiving its accruement," writes the artist Anne Truitt in *Turn*, one of her published journals. I fight back my own tears as the first measures of Mozart's Sonata No. 11 in A Major begin to play in my head. *Be who you needed when you were younger.* He reaches out a trembling hand, and I take it.

A group of us are on a friend's pontoon for an annual floating party during which their pontoon hooks up with another friend's pontoon in the middle of a lake. It's the golden hour, just before sunset. Prosecco is being poured—or tequila—take your pick. In this soft, summer light, everyone on the boat is as beautiful as they will ever be. It is impossible not to feel the good fortune of being here at this moment. The boat gently rocks. The hills surrounding the lake are glowing.

This friend—one of my nearest and dearest—has just bought a home on the lake on property that is distinguished by a long, private stretch of beach. As her husband steers the pontoon within view of the property, she points it out to me.

"Our grandchildren will play together on that beach," she says.

If I squint, I can see them. Three, four, five of

them—our grandchildren—running in the sand, crouched down with buckets, collecting pebbles at the water's lapping edge. She has the vision of it, I realize. She and her husband imagined that future when they decided on the house. Their kids are still in high school, but they are preparing for a time down the road—a time that will be here before we know it.

I look across the boat at M. He's wearing a blue button-down shirt, sleeves rolled up to his elbows. His white hair is whipping in the breeze off the lake, and he has on a pair of vintage Persols he once told me had been swiped from a dead Somali warlord.

Will we ever think much beyond tomorrow? Our lives are lived in increments of days, weeks, months—certainly not decades. What's on our calendars between now and Christmas? Has the check shown up at the post office? When will I finish my book? Is the famous comedian losing interest? Will the television pilot get picked up? Does M. need to make a trip to L.A. to show his face?

I cannot envision our old age. I wouldn't dare even hazard a guess. I think of couples we know who have been together for forty, fifty, sixty years. One such couple travels the world to attend performances of Wagner's Ring Cycle. Another couple goes to just about every Off-Broadway show: their third thing. I wonder whether M. and I will have the luxury of a third thing—a passion beyond our work and our boy. "I trim myself to the storm of time," Emerson wrote in "Terminus," a midlife poem in which he reflected on aging.

Our world will narrow as the storm of time washes over us. It will bleach us, expose our knots, whittle us down like old driftwood. It is this narrowing—not uncertainty—which is inevitable. The narrowing will not happen today, nor tomorrow. Not this year, nor next. Not this decade, nor—perhaps—the one after. There is luck involved, of course. But not only luck.

The pontoon continues to glide past the beach, leaving behind our future grandchildren and their small, curved backs as they forage for treasure. I want to call out to them. I wish I knew their names. I want to let them know that I intend to be on that beach, watching them from a spot in the shade.

When my father regained consciousness after their car crash, he had only one question: *Where is my wife?* Sometimes he recognized me or my half sister. Other times, he threw his bedclothes across the room, exposing himself. He yelled at nurses and orderlies. Though he had broken no bones in the accident—it seemed he'd had a stroke at the wheel—he was completely altered, a stranger. *Where is my wife?*

My parents were on different floors of the hospital. The doctors expressed grave concern that seeing my physically shattered mother might be too much of a shock to my terribly confused father. So we waited.

Each day I alternated between my parents' bedsides.
My mother asked about my father, too, but only
questions to which there were answers she could
bear. *He's going to be fine,* she would say, chin jutting
determinedly beneath her fractured cheekbones and
nose. *We're both going to be fine. You'll see.*

After a week, the doctors gave me permission to
wheel my father down to my mother's room. When
I let her know he'd be coming, she asked for a mirror
for the first time since the accident. She looked at her
ravaged face without saying a word. And then she
put on lipstick.

I brought my father to her. In the elevator, he
pressed every button within reach. He clutched a
Polaroid I had taken of her so he could be prepared
for the extent of her injuries. *Where is my wife?*
I moved his wheelchair right up to the rail of her bed.
Her eyes were huge as she looked at him.

Tears streamed down his face as he grabbed her
hand.

"We're fucked," he cried.

It was a word I had never heard him say.

"No, Paul. Everything's going to be fine."

"We're fucked," he cried again and again.

On the nineteenth anniversary of the night we met,
I'm upstairs in my office when M. starts to send me
e-mails from his office downstairs containing scanned

black-and-white photos taken at our wedding. *First scan. Second scan. Third scan.* The photos have been in a box for all these years.

In the first, we are under the chuppah. The smallest bit of fringe from my father's tallis is visible above us, and the rabbi's hands, holding open a prayer book, can be seen in a corner of the image. I am holding a goblet of wine to M.'s lips. The second photo looks like it was snapped late in the evening. M. is no longer wearing his jacket, and my hair has come loose from its updo. We're both looking away from the camera, and my guess is that we're cutting the cake.

Then another image comes through. This one M. has labeled *Private Moment* in the subject line. I open it and am transported back to the minutes before our wedding. We're upstairs at the small inn, where a handful of guests—a total of eighteen—are gathering below. The rabbi has asked us to write each other a letter, and M. has just given his to me. I am looking down at it—either taking it out of the envelope, or returning it, and my face is full of simple joy. M. leans toward me with his whole being. He's saying something. What is he saying? What did we write?

I forage through my entire office looking for those letters, which I recall putting together in a single envelope for safekeeping. I still have the dried flowers from my wedding bouquet in a vase on top of a bookcase. The white linen napkin containing the shards of broken glass from the end of our ceremony is tied with a ribbon and tucked into a drawer in our dining room cupboard. Our *ketubah*—our Hebrew wedding vows—is framed and hangs in the hall outside our bedroom.

I walk downstairs and find M. sitting in front of a scanner, our wedding photos spread across his desk.

"I'm making a wedding album," he says. *Nineteen years.*

"Do you have any idea where those letters are?" I ask. "The ones in the photo?"

"You have them," M. says.

I don't tell M. that I can't find the letters. Instead, I keep rooting through drawers and closets. I find the eulogy I wrote for my mother; Jacob's old report cards; my father's wallet. I find a stack of envelopes containing resolutions that M., Jacob, and I have written for the past six New Year's Eves. Not much has changed: Jacob wants to be taller than his dad. M. is intent on weighing one hundred and seventy-five pounds again. I want to live more fully in the moment.

I find notes from a phone session with a psychic referred to me by my literary agent during a time when I was scrambling and one of M.'s projects was falling apart: *You need a hug. No certainty. Gonna settle down. The truth is, you're scared. Caught up in what you think should happen. Everybody needs to take a breather. Wondering what is next?*

And finally, a note I made during a long conversation with my dear friend the Buddhist teacher who has been married sixty years: *The future—even minutes from now—is an actuarial guess.*

"Let everything happen to you: beauty and terror," Rilke wrote. Nearly a century later, the poet Elizabeth Alexander explores this in the wake of her husband Ficre's sudden death. "When we met those many years ago, I let everything happen to me, and it was beauty. Along the road, more beauty, and fear and struggle, and work, and learning, and joy. I could not have kept Ficre's death from happening, and from happening to us. It happened; it is a part of who we are; it is our beauty and our terror. We must be gleaners from what life has set before us."

A two-hour drive to Saint Rémy, where we then spent an hour finding the hotel. M. refused to ask directions. We had been fifty yards from the hotel the whole time. We got a room in a renovated carriage house— really renovated—and switching rooms became too difficult. We had a lovely time together but, well, the place bugged me. That night we went into town and had dinner at Bistrot des Alpilles, where there was an American family of four. I became transfixed by them. Father, mother, brother, sister? Or boyfriend, girlfriend? Or was the mother really the stepmother? I wanted to know. They were staying at our hotel—but

still, I never found out. I was struck by how well they
all got along.

M. seems very tired. Granted, the dogs wake him up
early—sometimes far too early. Yesterday, before
dawn, the big fluffy white one took off after a deer in
the darkness and M. had to chase him all the way down
our driveway. The upside, he told me later, was that
the sunrise was magnificent. *Fortunately, unfortunately.*

But I wonder if more than sleep deprivation is going
on. His Boston accent has been rising up within him,
as if some earlier version of himself is gaining ground.
As if—exhausted, depleted, disappointed—he might just
let the tsunami of time wash over him and carry him
away. *Are you here?* I sometimes want to take him by the
shoulders and shake him until he wakes up and I see the
light in his eyes. *You can't do this. You can't leave me alone.*

It's not that I'm afraid that he'll die. It's not that
I'm worried—as I know he is—that he will inherit the
Alzheimer's that runs through his mother's side of the
family. It's that I'm frightened that he will vanish in
plain sight. That he will lose hope. That his hands will
grow too stiff and heavy to roll the dice once more.
The man I met twenty years ago had already lived
more than one life, and he carried a world of pain
inside him. Somalia, Rwanda, Uganda, Sudan. The
battles, explosions, famines, deaths. The line of fire—
and all the reasons he put himself in the line of fire.

Once—years ago—at dinner in New Haven with a
South African friend, we listened as she told the story
of her father, a concert violinist, whose car ran off
the road in a remote part of South Africa while on his
way to play at a gig. He was badly injured, alone, and
no one discovered him for a couple of days. His legs
had to be amputated. Just after she finished telling the
story, M. excused himself and went to the men's room.
He was gone a long time. When he returned to the
table he looked pale, unwell, but he shook it off and
said he was fine.

It wasn't until much later—weeks, maybe months—
that he told me he had felt the world spinning as our
friend told the story. That he'd felt faint and vomited
in the men's room. Something in the barrenness of the
landscape; the solitary, grave injury; the staggering
aloneness of a man bleeding in the desert for days had
triggered a flashback to the horrors he had experienced
but never let himself feel.

"Maybe I should have kept doing it," M. recently said
to me, during a rare moment of looking backward.
He reminded me of the first year of our marriage,
when he was offered magazine assignments in the
Congo and Iraq. CNN called often and invited him
to appear as a talking head. He testified before the
Senate Foreign Relations Committee. Now he is
no longer in anyone's Rolodex. Now there are no

longer Rolodexes. We talked about the interest in a
book proposal that would have required him to spend
months in West Africa. Where would we be now if he
had taken the assignments, chosen to write the book?
It could have happened. / It had to happen.

Instead, he has walked a long way down this road
with me. The house, the yard, the wife, the boy, the
dogs, the schools, the quiet countryside. I believe he
doesn't regret it. But still, has being with me stopped
him from being him?

Two, three, four in the morning. I turn on my side and
watch M. as his chest rises and falls. *I'll take care of it,*
I silently tell him. *I'll take care of it.*

The Business, an inside-Hollywood radio show, ran
an episode ten years ago in which a screenwriter spoke
with the show's host about his career. The episode
is titled "The Almost Guy." The screenwriter had
enjoyed a quick and unusual ascent when he first
arrived on the scene. He signed with a powerful
agent, was offered blind script deals with multiple
television networks, and then—after a few years
in which a lot got written but nothing got made, a
"painful succession of high-level near misses"—his
career vaporized. "How far can talent, good looks, and
connections take you in Hollywood?" The producer

asks a rhetorical question during the show's opening teaser. "All the way to limbo."

"You've had more success than 99.9 percent of people who come to Hollywood," the producer muses. "But you haven't succeeded. Why? Is it you?"

"Yeah," the writer responds, his voice sounding worn thin. "You start to wonder."

M. and I listened to the episode shortly after it aired as we drove into the city early one morning. He had just turned fifty and things were looking pretty good. A script had been picked up by a major studio. The contracts were with the lawyers. An in-demand young director was attached. M. and the director had just returned from L.A., where they had lunch with Jim Carrey.

The two of us sped along the Saw Mill River Parkway. Every word the screenwriter said resonated: "I've given up on creative satisfaction, and now I'm just trying to pay the rent."

The business is cruel. We knew this. There are no guarantees. We'd been there. We felt bad for the guy. But we were going to be okay. We were going to get to have creative satisfaction *and* pay the rent. M. wove in and out of traffic, my hand on the back of his neck. Later that afternoon—on our way home from the city—we pulled into a Starbucks so M. could take a call from his agent.

"You know I don't say things like this—" she began.

And it was true. She didn't.

"—but you're going to win a statue for this script."

Some things that definitely won't happen: We won't have more children; we won't host big family reunions; we won't own a compound where generations will spend summer weekends playing badminton and roasting s'mores. Jacob won't grow up in the city. I won't enroll in a doctoral program to become a psychoanalyst, nor will I go to rabbinical school. M. and I will not move to Nairobi, where he will be based as a correspondent. He will not accept a job offer from the CIA, or the World Bank.

From fifty to eighty, Grace Paley said. *Seconds, not minutes.*

More difficult to contemplate are the things that *may* not happen. M. and I have each spent our lives doing work that—even when it succeeds—is subject to failure. ("Every novel is a failure," a great mentor once told me. At the time, I found this heartening.) Neither one of us chose an easy path, and that young couple wandering around the East Village may not

get the results they were counting on, the life they
bargained for, the one that seemed to spread out
before them like an orchard full of fruit ripe for the
taking.

A friend wins the Pulitzer Prize.

Another wins a MacArthur.

A Golden Globe, an Emmy, an Oscar.

Is this what we dared to hope for—these grand
ambitions? And if we dared—dare we still? Books,
essays, stories, films have built us a beautiful life, like
an image projected onto a screen, both real and unreal,
interruptible. For years, we gambled. Our stakes were
our very selves. *You were in luck—a rake, a hook, a
beam, a brake, a jamb, a turn, a quarter inch, an instant.*
For years we had the persistent sensation in our life
and art—John Updike's phrase—that we were just
beginning.

I am pleased, if startled, to see that M. and I have been
reunited as husband and wife. Right there, just beneath
my date and place of birth, he is listed as my spouse.
I search under his name and see that the problem
has been completely rectified. I wonder what finally
got Google to change its mind about our marriage.
Perhaps it was the words of a sixteen-year-old boy?
*I want to assure you that my parents are very much
together.* Or maybe all that data—thousands of bits and
bytes rearranged themselves to tell the story of two

people whose fates are so bound, each to the other, that there is no untangling them.

M. continues his scanning spree. He's rigged several old pieces of computer equipment together and has created a scanning station in his office. The wedding photos continue to crop up in my e-mail. Oh, how young we look! If I close my eyes, I can still hear the cello music—a friend of a friend from Juilliard—drift up the inn's stairs. My mother is there, looking regal in midnight-blue lace. Had malignant cells already begun to form a tumor deep in the soft tissue of her lung? A dear friend is hugging me. She and I will have a falling-out five years later and never speak again. The rabbi knocks on the door with the *ketubah* for us to sign. *Ani l'dodi v'dodi li*. I am my beloved, and my beloved is mine.

More photos keep pouring in. Hidden among the endless Alps captured on my parents' vacation slides is an image I have never seen before. On a glistening white beach I am a little girl beaming with unbridled joy on the lap of her father, a deeply tanned young man who looks at home in the world. I stare at the photo of my beautiful, lost father and the unself-conscious child whose whole self presses against him with the ease of knowing how absolutely she is loved. What happened? Where did that simple love go? As the calendar's battered pages flew by in a steady wind, sorrow overtook us both. That love was buried between us—and then buried with my father—but if I grow still, I can sense it as surely as I can hear the Prelude to Bach's Cello Suite No. 1. and feel the hug of the woman who is no longer my friend.

"My life is a museum," says my ninety-one-year-old aunt. "I can walk through any of the galleries at any time." My eighty-year-old Buddhist friend talks of receiving a digital picture frame as a gift—a device onto which thousands of images can be loaded. "I've seen the sun rise over Haleakala. I've been to the Dalai Lama's palace in Dharamsala. But I think that at the moment of my death, I'd like to be looking at those pictures of everyone I have ever loved."

M.'s mother is now a permanent resident of the memory unit in an assisted-living facility north of Boston. A few months ago she fell and broke her hip. The one-two punch of broken hip plus Alzheimer's is disastrous. She has been disoriented, in agony, drugged into a stupor. She will never get out of bed again.

The memory unit is housed in a sun-filled modern building by a lake. Its denizens are well-taken-care-of elderly people in the mid to late stages of Alzheimer's. The doors are locked, and a code is required to enter or exit. A group sits in a circle with a social worker, playing memory games:

"What is an underground train called?" she asks.

"The subway!" one of them calls out.

"How do you say 'sir' in Spanish?"

"Señor!"

Hardly anyone ever visits their relatives in the memory unit. Anyone, that is, except for M.'s family. In the ninety-four days since she fell, my father-in-law has been there ninety-three times. At first, he thought she'd get better. *Get up, sweetheart! You have to walk again! I need someone to make me breakfast!* But as the months have ticked by, now he simply comes and holds her hand. *Sixty years.*

It's Father's Day, and somehow I'm expecting this day to be different. I imagine the place will be full of families, but today is like any other. There's a skeleton staff, and the bright halls are eerily quiet. A man named Ralph sits in his khakis and soft burgundy cardigan, staring benignly into space. A woman is wheeled by, clutching two tattered Cabbage Patch dolls. But around M.'s mother's bed, a party is going on. We're there, as are M.'s brother, M.'s sister, M.'s brother's ex-wife. Jacob has come, and two of his cousins.

Just as it always was in my in-laws' house, it's loud. There's laughing and cursing and roll-your-eyes impropriety. In the midst of it, my mother-in-law struggles through her methadone haze. She is being spoon-fed by her ex-daughter-in-law. Her husband is by her side. She mumbles, so for a moment it's hard to make out what she's saying: *Everyone I love is all around me.*

According to the English moral philosopher Mary Midgley, "We *are* each not only one but also many. Might this fact deserve a little more philosophic attention? Some of us have to hold a meeting every time we want to do something only slightly difficult, in order to find the self who is capable of undertaking it . . . We spend a lot of time and ingenuity on developing ways of organizing the inner crowd, securing consent among it, and arranging for it to act as a whole. Literature shows that the condition is not rare."

Dig deep enough and everything that has ever happened is alive and whole, a world unto itself— scenes, words, images—unspooling in some other dimension. I am not referring to memory, but rather, to a galaxy that exists outside the limited reach of memory. It can be understood, perhaps, as the place where neurobiology ends and physics begins. The law of conservation of energy states that the total energy of an isolated system remains constant—it is said to be conserved over time.

All those selves—that inner crowd—clamor inside me. The girl who believed men would save her. The young woman who made harsh and quick work of

herself—*savage obstinacy*—and nearly succeeded in
her blind, flailing quest for self-ruin. The one who
said *I do,* and then didn't. The one who kept journals
despite it all. The one who turned over the shovelful
of earth and heard it hit the plain pine box six feet
below—once, twice. The one who said *I do,* then
did. The one who wrote books as if her life depended
on it. The one who held her baby to her breast and
sang *Hush little baby, don't you cry.* The one who was
going to save him or die trying. The one who fled the
city after the towers fell. The one who grew up. The
one—now—with her boy on the verge of manhood,
her man struggling with his own wounded spirit, who
is consumed with a sense of urgency. *From fifty to
eighty.*

Somewhere, a clock ticks. Sand pours through the
hourglass. I am no longer interested in the stories but
rather, what is underneath the stories: the soft, pulsing
thing that is true. Why now? What is this insistence?
All of me—the whole crowd—wants to know.

I rarely walk into the room I cleared out. The futon
sits on its simple, elegant frame. A standing paper
lantern that belonged to my mother occupies one
corner. I thought I needed an empty room—a room
of my own, not cluttered with matters of work and
family life. A space in which I could just *be,* not push
myself in this direction or that one. I was certain I

would meditate each morning on that futon, that I would practice yoga in the silence, behind a door that was mine and mine alone.

Instead, I hover at the threshold of the room and admire it. So clean! So spacious! Not a dust mote, nor a smudge, a small fingerprint mars its pristine emptiness. Once, I longed for such emptiness. *We were young, and in the reproductive years.* Now part of me longs for the chaos: the call of my name across the house in a high, piercing voice: *Mom!* The weekends jam-packed with games, matches, recitals, school plays. In the silence, I hear beyond the immediate: a siren a mile away; the caw of a crow; M. making a fresh pot of coffee downstairs. Oh, and our friendly woodpecker, of course. *Rat-tat-tat.*

"You do not know the road," offers Berry. "You have committed your life to a way."

Tacked to the wall in the empty room, opposite the single lamp, is a piece of brown construction paper that stretches from ceiling to floor. On the paper is the outline of a woman, life-sized, crudely traced in black magic marker. The lines show where her hair fans out, shoulders, arms, fingers. Her torso, waist, thighs, legs, and feet. Some women writer friends outlined each other one night after dinner at an artists' colony—it began as a lark but turned into something powerful: a sense that we were showing each other where we begin and where we end.

Sometimes I wander into the room and contemplate

my outline, floating as she does, a few inches off the
ground. She reminds me of a grown-up version of the
paper dolls I used to play with as a girl. I used to dress
those paper dolls in preparation for their future lives,
the selves they might someday become. There were
so many options! An evening gown, surgical scrubs,
a wedding dress, a bikini. But this life-sized drawing is
unadorned, just a swooping, unbroken line encircling
all of me. If I laid her flat on the floor, she might look
like a chalk outline from a crime scene. Or a snow
angel. She might look like anything at all.

That night at the artists' colony, each of us took
turns resting on the cool, damp floor of the barn as the
others knelt by our sides as if performing a sacred rite.
There were seven of us. We ranged in age from forty
to eighty-four. Among us, we had written twenty-
nine books. Had seven children. Ten marriages. We
were single, widowed, divorced. We lived in cities and
on remote islands. We were struggling, contented,
bewildered, joyful, full of longing, grief-stricken,
fearful, searching, at peace.

When we had finished all the outlines, we dragged
them out of the barn and placed them in a row in a
field. It was a cool night, the setting sun low in the sky.
Some of us took out our phones and snapped pictures.
What had happened here? What were these shapes on
the brown paper, on the grass? What did it mean—
we wondered—to have become us?

· ·

A few years ago, a graphic designer named Maya Eilam created a colorful infographic in blue, black, and orange tones, inspired by a rejected graduate school thesis written in 1947 by Kurt Vonnegut. Vonnegut contended that there are four basic plots in life which can be given shape by graphing them. His illustrations were dry and linear, but in Eilam's interpretation, the basic plots become curvy, playful dances between happy outcomes and sad ones. The symbols for happy outcomes are butterflies, babies, angels, trophies, treble notes, shining suns. The symbols for somewhat-less-happy outcomes are thunderclouds, syringes, hospital beds, bombs, skulls.

The four basic plots as shown in Eilam's infographic: *Man in Hole,* in which the main character gets into trouble, then gets out of it again and ends up better off for the experience; *Boy Meets Girl,* in which the main character comes across something wonderful, gets it, loses it, then gets it back forever; *From Bad to Worse,* in which the main character starts off poorly, then gets continually worse with no hope for improvement; and finally, *Which Way Is Up?*—the plot most difficult to graph—in which the story has a lifelike ambiguity that keeps us from knowing if new developments are good or bad.

As a young writer I became friendly with the author and naturalist Peter Matthiessen, who at the time I met him was in his late seventies and had written

twenty-two books. He was about to publish a new
novel, a book of which he was particularly proud.
"The early books aren't worth reading," he told me
with a wave of his hand, as if swatting away a few
pesky flies. At the time, I had written the same number
of books—three—that Matthiessen was dismissing.
I couldn't imagine ever feeling that way. My whole
self had gone into those books. But sure enough—
a few books later, I found myself saying something
similar to my students. "Don't read the early work,"
I'd tell them—shrugging off a decade. Even my more
recent books present me with some small measure of
embarrassment.

The span of years! The selves we shed and shed—
only to have them rise within us once more. When
Philip Roth retired—telling the world he had put
down his pen for good—he set out to reread his entire
oeuvre in order to decide for himself whether any of it
had been worthwhile. I wonder if he did this. And—if
so—I wonder what he found.

My ninety-one-year-old aunt (*ninety-one and a
half,* she says) calls on the morning of M.'s sixtieth
birthday. We're laying low—no big party, no forced
celebration. M. has been sitting all morning in his
white bathrobe at the kitchen table, scrolling through
birthday wishes on Facebook. I had woken up thinking
about M.'s fiftieth. That script had just sold. His

agent told him he was going to win a statue. I threw him a big party at a friend's Tribeca loft—the mood buoyant, bordering on triumphant. *Finally, finally.*

My aunt asks after Jacob, and I give her news of my boy, all of it good. He's on the honor roll, in the school play, playing varsity tennis. He's genuinely happy and engaged by his life. As I've lately been saying, *It's good to be Jacob.* These years are ones I don't think he'll long to dismiss someday. They are building blocks—solid steps he's taking in becoming his next self, and his next.

This morning Jacob posted a photo of the three of us—along with his birthday wishes to his father—on Instagram. He chose one of my favorites. We're sitting on the stone steps leading to our house, my head on M.'s shoulder. Jacob—perhaps he is four—has his little arms slung around M.'s neck. And M. is looking straight at the camera with a small smile.

Now my aunt is asking about M., and I hear my own voice quaver as I strive for equilibrium. She loves M., and I don't want to burden her. I tell her about M.'s struggles—his third rewrite of the television pilot, the postponement with the comedian—and can feel her listening carefully on the other end of the phone. And then she asks: *How are his spirits?*

Before I know what's happened, tears are rolling down my cheeks. That gentle question—*how are his spirits?*—has unleashed in me a sorrow so intense that I am unable to contain it. Because the answer is that M.

is injured and I can't fix things for him. No, it's more than that. I'm part of his injury, a perpetrator of it. Sometimes it feels like his leg is caught in a trap. If he hadn't left Africa. If he hadn't become a filmmaker. If he hadn't become a father. If he hadn't met me. I'm sure he wonders every single day whether—in the end—he will have missed his mark. But the infinitely more troubling question is whether—having missed his mark—he will also have lost himself.

"You know," my aunt says, "I once had a terribly difficult period that lasted twenty-four years." Wait. *Twenty-four years?* "And it was so important to realize that I didn't know what was on the other side of the darkness. Every so often there was a sliver of light that shot the whole world through with mystery and wonder, and reminded me: I didn't have all the information."

"An honorable human relationship in which two people have the right to use the word 'love,'" Adrienne Rich wrote, "is a process, delicate, violent, often terrifying to both persons involved, a process of refining the truths they can tell each other."

Driving home from Woodstock, New York—alone in my car—I crank the volume on the satellite radio. I'm tuned into my regular station, the Bridge, which seems

to play Fleetwood Mac every five songs, Jackson
Browne every six, with a smattering of Jim Croce,
Elton John, and Neil Young in between.

The narrow road takes me past horse farms,
orchards, a herd of cows grazing in a pasture. Ever
since moving to the country, these kinds of drives
are my favorite time to think. When Jacob was a
little boy—even up until this year when he got his
learner's permit—the car was where we had our best
conversations. Hands on the wheel, eyes on the road.
And M. and I have spent countless companionable
hours together—M. driving, always—on our round
trips to the city early in the morning, late at night.
But this solitary time is like a meditation. Thoughts,
feelings, rise to the surface, fall away.

The voices of Carly Simon and James Taylor
fill the car. It's 1978 and they're singing "Devoted
to You."

> *Darling you can count on me*
> *Till the sun dries up the sea.*
> *Until then I'll always be*
> *Devoted to you.*

I choke back the tears that seem to be close to the
surface these days. They were so young. So in love.
Weren't they?

When I get home, I watch a YouTube video of
the two of them singing the song on *The Dick Cavett*

Show. She's wearing white pants and a simple pale sweater. He's in a plaid button-down shirt and cradles his guitar. She's holding a microphone, leaning toward him, singing to him. He's looking straight ahead, strumming the guitar.

Why isn't he looking at her? It isn't until the end of the song that he meets her eye and blurts out a couple of words I had to play back again to be sure I heard correctly. *Sobering sentiment.* Were they already in trouble? Was he wasted? Had he started cheating on her? They divorced six years later. The first viewer comment in the chain below the video reads: *She was so beautiful. If I was James, I would have looked at her and sang it like I meant it.*

A friend writes me a note about a book she's just finished. It's an academic treatise on female memoirists, and she assumes I'm familiar with it. I am not. "But you're in it," she tells me. "There's a whole chapter about you."

I find the chapter and read it with interest. The author explores my first memoir through a feminist, politicized lens, describing it as "a formidable journey toward self-reliance."

But then it all falls apart. She is bitterly let down by the wording of my acknowledgments, which casts the book in a "not just dubious but downright disappointing" light by suggesting a fairy-tale ending in which I have found my handsome prince. This is a first. I had never considered acknowledgments up for review. The disappointing words—the final paragraph after I thank friends, family, agents, and editors—were these: "Most of all, my husband, M., who helped me feel safe, read every word, and made me believe in happily ever after."

Le Grand-Hôtel du Cap-Ferrat is very grand in the impossibly luxurious manner of the Côte d'Azur. We lounged by the gorgeous pool with its infinity edge overlooking the Mediterranean. I read Falconer. *M. was reading Arundhati Roy's novel. Got a bit sunburned. We spent most of the afternoon in bed. Later, we went to the bar (named after Somerset Maugham—no one knows why) and hung out with the pink-suited, pink-cheeked, snowy-white-hair brigade. Then we ordered a club sandwich from room service and kept doing what we had been doing all afternoon.*

On the day Jacob will be taking his driver's license test, I'm making coffee in the kitchen when I hear a little boy laughing. I know that boy's laugh. I will know it forever. M. calls me up to his office, where he is continuing his archival project that began with the scans of our wedding photos—though the album has yet to materialize—and has now moved to hundreds of hours of video.

Here's my tiny boy on M.'s computer monitor, picking the marshmallows out of a plastic bowl of Lucky Charms. He has a head of blond curls and the biggest eyes I've ever seen. He's wearing blue flannel pajamas. His lips are rosebuds. And here's M., turning the camera so both of them are in the frame. *Who's that?* M. asks. His voice is so patient and kind. *Who are those two guys?* Jacob isn't having any of it. He's reaching for the camera. *I want to put my eye there,* he says, pointing to the viewfinder.

I stand just behind M. as we watch the screen. I feel as if I might explode with tenderness. Then, now. Here is Jacob in our basement before we renovated it, riding around on a plastic tricycle. *I'm a run-around, run-around, run-around kid. I'm a fly-around, fly-around, fly-around kid.* The song lyrics are as indelible as the prayers I learned at my father's knee. And here I am, lighting the Hanukkah candles in our kitchen, Jacob in my arms.

And here is our handsome, young man in his corduroys and Patagonia, aching for the moment of freedom today represents. *I'm a drive-around, drive-around, drive-around kid.* After passing the test with ease, he takes our car to a nearby town to meet friends for dinner and a movie. M. and I watch as the taillights recede down the driveway, past the rope swing, past the best sledding hill, until we can no longer see him.

It's a cold, early winter night. M. will light a fire in the fireplace. I will open a bottle of wine and boil some ravioli. Our plan is to read applications for our conference in Italy: a third thing. We'll sit by the fire and talk about language, intention, talent, generosity, openness, courage. *Listen to this line,* one of us may say. *How about this?*

What we will not talk about: that young woman lighting Hanukkah candles, that dark-haired man holding his toddler aloft, and the dreams they have both built and broken together. We will not ask each other about the truths we have yet to refine. We understand that suffering and happiness are no longer individual matters. Tonight, we will stay at the edge of the dark forest until—together—we are brave enough to go back inside.

M. and I pay a visit to Donald Hall in the New Hampshire farmhouse where he lived in "double solitude" with Jane Kenyon for most of their marriage, and where he has remained for the past two decades since her death. Don is eighty-four. He stopped shaving some years after Jane died, on the suggestion of a young lover who thought he would look Mephistophelian—which he does. He has written that he enjoys being grubby and noticeable.

The third things he shared with Jane Kenyon are all around. The volumes of Keats on the sagging bookshelves; Chekhov; Elizabeth Bishop; the manuscripts, literary journals piled to table height.

The peak of Mount Kearsarge is visible in the distance.
Across Route 4, a two-lane country road, is Eagle
Pond, where they spent late-summer afternoons on a
small private beach under the shade of white pines and
ghost birches, reading, swimming, taking notes.

Eagle Pond was a third thing they lost to leakage
from a landfill that turned the pond stinky and orange.
Sometimes you lose a third thing. As M. and I sit with
him in the waning afternoon light—his house lit by
a single lamp, shadows falling across the darkening
rooms—I bring up Eagle Pond. I wonder aloud what
happens when something so integral to a couple is lost.

The poet's eyes twinkle and he smiles at me.

"Well, sometimes you get it back."

M.'s manager calls. The pilot is genius. The famous
comedian's schedule has opened up. Financing is
imminent. M. is not so interested in the praise. He
knows that Hollywood is a place in which it is entirely
possible, as Dorothy Parker put it, to die from
encouragement. But there is some reason for hope—
fortunately, unfortunately—and so I do. I hope. *We've
been here before*, M. says. But no. The very sentence is
an impossibility. We've never been *here*, before.

After M. and I finish the play for the pharmaceutical
company and it has been vetted by attorneys, scien-

tists, doctors, and several marketing teams, it becomes the centerpiece of a day-long program designed to create empathy for Alzheimer's patients and their caregivers. M. and I are invited to take part in a project conceived by a geriatric specialist called the Virtual Dementia Tour.

In a large conference room at their suburban New Jersey headquarters, we each take off our shoes and are given a pair of sandals, soles fitted with sharp plastic spikes. Alzheimer's can cause neuropathy— a constant pinpricking sensation in the patient's feet. I think of the way my mother-in-law used to shuffle.

We're asked to put on several pairs of plastic surgical gloves. The disease slows motor function and dims vision. Over our eyes, goggles with scratched lenses the color of urine. But the calling card of the disease is, of course, that it steals memory. A lifetime's cache of images, stories, experiences, deleted one pixel at a time, as if a virus were erasing a hard drive. *What can I tell you? I'm still crazy about the sonofabitch.*

Massive headphones are placed over our ears. Blaring bits of static, music, snatches of dialogue, random, electronic sounds: a car door slamming, a ticking clock, a siren, all overlaid as if by a maniac spinning a radio dial. M. stands next to me, but I can barely make out his expression through the scratched yellow goggles. I reach for his hand but can't feel it through the layers of surgical gloves.

We are each given a separate set of instructions—

a list of five simple tasks. We've been strictly prohib-
ited from asking for the list to be repeated. As hard
as I strain to listen through the din of the headphones,
I'm able to make out only three of my tasks. *Sort pills,*
I hear. *Write note to family. Fold blanket.* M. is then led
away from me. I can do nothing but watch him go.
We are not allowed to take the Virtual Dementia Tour
together.

Sometimes I think I have organized the inner crowd.
For a brief, breathtaking moment, I feel completely
whole. I understand that I am composed of many
selves that make up a single chorus. To listen to the
music this chorus makes, to recognize it as music, as
something noble, varied, patterned, sublime—that is
the work of a lifetime.

"Let the young soul look back upon its life and ask
itself: what until now have you truly loved, what has
raised up your soul, what ruled it and at the same time
made it happy? Line up these objects of reverence
before you, and perhaps by what they are and their
sequence, they will yield you a law, the fundamental
law of your true self." These words, from Nietzsche's
Unmodern Observations, are the last in my latest
commonplace book.

Sort pills. Write note to family. Fold blanket. I am alone.
Alone in a dark, unfamiliar room filled with piles

and piles of stuff, reminiscent of a neglected storage
locker. I know researchers are observing me from
behind one-way glass—that this is an experiment in
empathy, that we are, in fact, on the sprawling campus
of a pharmaceutical company in New Jersey, that I
can rip off the headphones at any moment and return
to my present life, my *real* life—but this offers me
no comfort. I can barely see through the goggles. My
feet hurt. Every step is agony, the sharp plastic spikes
digging into my soles. *Sort pills. Write note to family.*
Fold blanket. I try to make out the shapes around me.
I see an ironing board, a stack of sweaters. A ball of
twine. My determination to cross items off any to-do
list—always a strong suit of mine—feels slippery.
Suddenly, I am a child playing hide-and-seek in
the dark. Counting. Eyes squeezed shut. Terrified.
Wondering if anyone will ever find me.

Blanket. Pills. Note. I keep repeating the words
like a prayer so I can remember them through the
terrible din. The inside of my head is a needle against
a scratched record, skipping, skipping. I feel my way
around a cluttered table. A pill case! I try to pick it up.
I barely feel it in the palm of my hand. After several
tries, I get it open. Then I begin to sort the pills as
best I can. Most of them spill to the floor, and I am
suddenly, irrationally furious.

I move around the table, supporting myself on my
hands to take the pressure off my feet. I push an iron
out of the way, a magazine, a wooden hanger. The
notebook. I find the notebook. My gloved fingers

won't close around a pencil, so I hold it the way a child would, in my fist. By now it all feels nearly futile. I'm on the verge of tears. What is the last task? Through the static, I remember: the blanket. I have to fold it.

By now I'm dizzy, depleted. What difference can it possibly make? Who cares? I do a shitty job of folding the blanket and then—then I just sit down in a chair and wait for M. to rescue me.

The letters M. and I had exchanged before our wedding seem to have vanished. I empty the contents of drawers and folders, but the cream-colored envelope—I remember it so clearly—is nowhere to be found. It isn't like me to misplace something so important.

"Would you look again?" I ask M. "I'm pretty sure you put it somewhere."

"I remember we read them to each other on some anniversary," M. says. Seventh? Twelfth? Fourteenth?

"Check wherever you keep our marriage license."

An hour later, M. comes upstairs to my office, envelope in hand. Indeed, he had slipped it into a file in his office closet that also contained our marriage license, as well as both secular and religious divorce papers from my two earlier marriages.

"I haven't opened it," he says, handing it to me.

I don't open it either. I'm not quite ready to meet that bride and groom at the start of their lives together. Instead, I leave it on my desk atop a small pile of commonplace books. Two days later we were off on our honeymoon. *Day One: Took a walk around Saint-Germain, wound up in a small pizzeria off Rue de Seine. Pretty zonked. Went on search for le Tums.*

Our rabbi had given us an assignment I no longer remember. We had hardly known the rabbi. I had wanted a woman to officiate at our wedding, and we chose her out of a directory. In a few years, I will visit her when my baby is mortally ill. Later, she will bury my mother. Still later, I will be on bed rest, desperately trying to hold on to a second child whose heartbeat is already faint inside me. I will weep on the phone to her and she—who had just adopted a child from Guatemala—will listen hard and provide a sisterly compassion I will never forget. What promises did M. and I make to each other on our wedding day? What promises have we broken? And what promises have we kept?

Finally, on a quiet morning—the dogs snoring at my feet—I slide two pieces of paper from the envelope. M.'s is on proper stationery. He must have bought it especially for the occasion. Mine is a ripped-out page from my datebook.

Dearest M., I treasure you for your kindness, for your wisdom, for the fact that everything you have been through in your life has only made you a better person.

It all comes back to me. The rabbi had asked each of us to write what we treasure in the other. (Treasure \ verb: cherish; hold dear; prize; value greatly; adore; dote on; love, be devoted to, worship, venerate.) *I treasure you for the way you open me up, and the way I know we will only keep opening up, keep growing with each other all our lives.*

A few moments later—my father's yellowed tallis draped above us—I shook from head to toe as M. and I exchanged our vows. My heart was pounding so hard I thought I might die at my own wedding. I kept my eyes on M. *There you are.* "I have been taken by surprise by the recent events of my life," Anne Truitt wrote at the age of sixty-five, "but this can only be because I have not been alert to the signs that in retrospect intimate their direction. If I could tune in now, the future would be as legible as the past."

Dani, The moment you first looked at me I saw our future in your eyes. I felt the presence of an extraordinary force, something solid yet light. I treasure the way you say to me, "This is just the beginning." I want to hear you say it in ten years, in twenty, and thirty.

But I can no longer say to M. that we're just beginning. *Let everything happen to you: beauty and terror.* That solid yet light thing—our journey—is

no longer new. He identified my mother's body. We
took turns holding our seizing child. We have watched
his mother disappear in plain sight. We have raised
Jacob together. We know each other in a way that
young couple couldn't have imagined. Our shared
vocabulary—our own language—will die with us.
We are the treasure itself: fathoms deep, in the world
we have made and made again.

Alaska. At the end of a week of teaching—this time
on a refurbished crabbing vessel off the coast of
Homer—M., Jacob, and I were about to head back
home. The trip had been full of adventure: whale-
watching, seals, otters, and the bears that we knew
were all around us.

But a severe storm had blown in, and the bay
between the island and the mainland was turbulent,
the sky a deep gray crisscrossed by jagged flashes
of lightning. A harsh wind howled. The water
taxi bobbed violently at the dock as the three of us
staggered against the heavy rain, dragging our luggage
along the uneven planks.

I turned to the owner of the lodge.

"You've taken the water taxi in storms this bad,
right?"

She squinted over the bay.

"Nope. Not this bad."

We loaded our suitcases into the water taxi's small

interior cabin. A few other passengers were on board, local residents on their way to the mainland. One man was wearing hunting gear. His beagle cowered in a corner. The side of the boat banged against the dock. The captain looked tense. I wasn't at all sure we should be making this trip. But reconsidering wasn't a possibility. As soon as we were on board, we were under way.

The trip was havoc. The waves were eight feet high in the middle of the bay. We were airborne once, twice, slamming back down into the water so hard it seemed the boat might splinter. The porthole near Jacob's seat fogged up, and when the captain asked him to wipe it clear, an out-of-control leisure boat was bearing down on us. It seemed a distinct possibility that we all might perish. My family drowning in a storm off the coast of Alaska was not something I had ever considered. Later—once safely on the other side—our fellow passengers told us that in all their years of making that trip they had never experienced anything like it.

It's a good story now. A good storm-at-sea story. Jacob likes to tell it. But when I think of that harrowing hour, it isn't the wild ride that stays with me so much as the moment we pulled away from the island. A group of my students had come to see us off, and they were huddled in bright yellow slickers, waving madly. Jacob and I found seats in the cabin and braced ourselves for the ride. I pinned one of my legs over his

to hold him down as we edged away from the dock.
Through the porthole I could see M. standing on the
boat's bow, lashed by rain. He held on to nothing.
He pointed his camera at the dock, the wild crashing
waves, finding beauty in the bright huddle.

After the Virtual Dementia Tour the assembled group
of one hundred or so executives sits in plush seats
in a well-appointed theater on the campus of the
pharmaceutical company to hear the results of the
experiment in empathy. Those of us who participated
have been observed and evaluated. The researcher
who speaks is careful not to divulge the identities of
the subjects but goes through the data that have been
collected.

Quite a number of us became frustrated or angry.
A few, like me, gave up. But there is one man the
researcher focuses on. This man broke the rules. He
insisted that the list of tasks be repeated until he was
sure he had heard them all.

This man took care of task after task, until he
arrived at the last item on his list: *put batteries in
flashlight and turn flashlight on.* He found the flashlight
and the batteries, managed after several attempts
to insert them. But the flashlight didn't work. The
batteries were in the wrong way. So he had to start
all over again. He unscrewed the flashlight and the
batteries fell to the floor. He got down on his knees

and rummaged until he found them. Then he held them in his gloved hands—but he couldn't see or feel which way they should go. So he took a battery and put it on his tongue. He licked the battery. Then he replaced them in the flashlight and stumbled to his feet. He switched the flashlight on—my husband— and raised his fists in victory.

Already my mind is a kaleidoscope. Years vanish. Months collapse. Time is like a tall building made of playing cards. It seems orderly until a strong gust of wind comes along and blows the whole thing skyward. Imagine it: an entire deck of cards soaring like a flock of birds. A song comes on the radio and now I am nursing my baby to sleep, his sweet little body heavy in my arms. I am at a crowded party near Gramercy Park, looking into his father's eyes for the first time. I am burying my own father. My mother. I am a girl watching her mother at her vanity table. I am holding M.'s hand at Jacob's college graduation. I am playing with my grandchildren in a house on a mountain. The phone rings. The doorbell. I understand something terrible with a thud in my heart. The plane, the car, the train, the bomb. The test results are ominous. I am wheeling M. down a corridor. We are playing golf in Arizona. We are homeless. We are living in Covent Garden, where we often attend the theater. Pick a card. Any card.

Day sixteen. Left Cap-Ferrat at the crack of dawn. Long layover in London. We took off from Heathrow. D. was feeling nervous at the end of this glorious honeymoon—so when, shortly after take-off, the captain announced that we were turning around due to an unspecified problem but first had to circle over the ocean to dump twenty tons of fuel before landing—and then, on our approach, when the plane was struck by lightning—D. had a bit of a meltdown. We got off the plane—M. was a prince—and got ourselves booked on a flight the next morning. We spent the very last night of our honeymoon eating Big Macs and making love in an airport hotel.

Day seventeen.
  Married.
  Home.

ALSO BY

Dani Shapiro

FAMILY HISTORY

Rachel Jensen is perfectly happy: in love with her husband, devoted to their daughter, Kate, gratified by her work restoring art. And finally, she's pregnant again. But as Rachel discovers, perfection can unravel in an instant. The summer she is thirteen, Kate returns from camp sullen, angry, and withdrawn. Everyone assures Rachel it's typical adolescent angst. But then Kate has a terrifying accident with her infant brother, and the ensuing guilt brings forth a dreadful lie—one that ruptures their family, perhaps irrevocably. *Family History* is a mesmerizing journey through the mysteries of adolescent pain and family crisis.

Fiction

BLACK & WHITE

Clara Brodeur has spent her entire adult life pulling herself away from her famous mother, the renowned and controversial photographer Ruth Dunne, whose towering reputation rests on the unsettling nude portraits she took of her young daughter. At age eighteen, sick of her notoriety as "the girl in the pictures," Clara fled New York City, settling and making her own family in small-town Maine. But years later, when Ruth reaches out from her deathbed, Clara suddenly finds herself drawn back to the past she thought she had escaped. This is a spellbinding novel that asks: How do we forgive those who failed to protect us?

Fiction

ANCHOR BOOKS
Available wherever books are sold.
www.anchorbooks.com